MY BIG BOOK OF science

OVER 60 EXCITING EXPERIMENTS TO BOOST YOUR STEM SCIENCE SKILLS

SUSAN AKASS

CICO Kidz

Published in 2019 by CICO Books
An imprint of Ryland Peters & Small Ltd
20–21 Jockey's Fields, London WC1R 4BW
341 E 116th St, New York, NY 10029

www.rylandpeters.com

10 9 8 7 6 5 4 3 2 1

A CIP catalog record for this book is available from
the Library of Congress and the British Library.

ISBN: 978 1 78249 747 9

Printed in China

Editor: Dawn Bates
Designer: Alison Fenton
Illustrators: Rachel Boulton and Hannah George

In-house designer: Eliana Holder
Art director: Sally Powell
Production controller: Mai-Ling Collyer
Publishing manager: Penny Craig
Publisher: Cindy Richards

contents

CHAPTER 3
amazing bodies

CHAPTER 4
outside science

setting up your science lab

Each experiment in the book includes a list of the ingredients or chemicals, materials, and other equipment you will need. Most of the materials can be found in the kitchen cabinet, but for some experiments you may have to buy or find something special, either from a drug store (pharmacy) or online.

We've listed below the items that you will need regularly, and which will be useful to have in your science lab. Some of the materials are things that you can reuse, perhaps from the recycling bin, or everyday things found around your home. Look out for them (ask before you take!) and build up your collection.

CHEMICALS: SCIENTIFIC INGREDIENTS

- Acrylic paint
- Baking powder
- Baking soda (bicarbonate of soda)
- Bubble mix (see below)
- Corn starch (cornflour)
- Dish soap (washing-up liquid): In the US, use Joy or Dawn; in the UK and Europe, use Fairy Liquid and Yes
- Dried yeast
- Food coloring
- Glycerin
- Liquid detergent
- Shaving foam (budget brands are best)
- Sugar
- Sugar-free soda
- Vinegar

Making bubble mix

Homemade bubble mix is stronger than store-bought and it's very simple to make. Simply pour about ½ cup (250 ml) warm water into a bowl. Add a tablespoon of glycerin or granulated sugar and 2 tablespoons of dish soap (washing-up liquid). Stir until all the sugar has dissolved. Try not to make any foam on the top. Cover the bowl tightly with plastic wrap and let it rest for several hours—the longer, the better.

SAFETY EQUIPMENT

- Two pairs of safety goggles
- Latex gloves

OTHER MATERIALS

- Balloon pump (optional but easier than blowing up balloons yourself)
- Balloons (including some long ones and some black and white ones)
- Bamboo skewers
- Bubble wrap
- Bubble wands: a round bubble wand and pipette bubble wand (cut the top off the bulb end)
- Chenille stems (pipe cleaners)
- Coffee filter papers
- Cookie cutters
- Cotton twine or string
- Dowel
- Drinking straws
- Elastic bands
- Fishing line or kite string
- Funnel
- Garden wire or wire coat hangers
- Hex nuts and bolts
- Marbles
- Paper clips
- Paper towels
- Plastic bottles (all sizes)
- Plastic cups
- Plastic pipettes
- Plastic wrap (clingfilm)
- PVA glue
- Sandpaper
- Sticky tack
- Soda can
- Strainer/sieve
- Strong paper, cardboard, or cardstock
- Strong sticky tape
- Thumb tacks (drawing pins)
- Ziplock bags

EXPERIMENT LEVELS

LEVEL 1
These are quick and easy experiments.

LEVEL 2
These experiments are quite easy but take
a little longer to complete.

LEVEL 3
These experiments are advanced techniques
and may need help from an adult.

SAFETY FIRST!

Science can be dangerous. Chemicals can react together in
unexpected ways and cause explosions or splash into your
eyes or onto your skin. If you use heat or fire, you can burn
yourself. That's why scientists take safety very seriously.

The experiments in this book are not dangerous,
but you should still learn to keep yourself safe.
Where there is any risk that you could hurt yourself,
the book tells you to ask an adult to help (look for
the safety symbol shown above). Make sure that
you do, and also, wear safety goggles when told
to—especially when popping balloons—then
you will both protect your eyes and really look
like a scientist!

science investigations

Each of the experiments in this book shows you how to do something that gives exciting results and then tells you what happened, using simple science.

That may be enough for you, but real scientists don't just follow instructions. They ask questions and then try to find out the answers for themselves. So, if you want to be a real scientist, do some more investigating, either by following the suggestions in "Let's Investigate," or by thinking of your own questions. A good question may lead you to carrying out a proper scientific fair test. To do this you will need to:

a) Ask a scientific question.
b) Make a prediction—what do you think will happen and why?
c) Carry out a fair test and make accurate and repeated measurements.
d) Record (write down) your results.
e) Reach a conclusion (decide if your results match your prediction or show something else).

A FAIR TEST
Let's take a simple bobbing raisin experiment as an example. Pour some soda into a tall glass. Drop a handful of raisins into the glass. Watch them carefully. After a few seconds they begin to dance— rising to the surface and then dropping back again. You can do various investigations to find out what makes the raisins bob more or less.

1 First list all the things you could change in the experiment (these are called variables), which might change how the raisins bob. These would be:
- *Size of glass*
- *Type of soda*
- *Level of soda in the glass*
- *Temperature of the soda*
- *Fizziness of the soda (how long the top has been off the soda bottle)*
- *Size of the raisins*

2 Now choose one of these variables to investigate by asking a scientific question that you can test. For that you need to think, "What can I measure or count?" Well, you could count how many times a raisin bobs to the surface in one minute, so your question could be:
Do the smaller raisins bob to the surface more often than the bigger raisins?

3 A good scientist then predicts the answer, with a reason. You might say:
"I think big raisins will bob less often because they need more bubbles around them to lift them to the surface because they are heavier."

4 Next, plan your test. To make it a fair test you can only change the variable you are investigating: The size of the raisin. The other variables (the glass, the soda, the level, the temperature, and the fizziness) must stay exactly the same. So your plan would be:
a) I will do the test three times—once with currants (which are like small raisins), once with ordinary raisins, and once with jumbo raisins, keeping all the other variables the same.
b) I will use a minute timer and count the number of times each raisin bobs to the surface of a glass of soda in one minute.
c) I will make a tally chart and mark it each time a raisin comes to the surface.

You will need more than one of each type of raisin because not all raisins behave in exactly the same way. One jumbo raisin might bob a lot of times and another not so many. Three of each kind would be a good number to use—with more it would be hard to count the bobs.

Imagine if you didn't keep the other variables the same. Say, for example, you counted raisins in cold soda and jumbo raisins in warm soda—how would you know if it was the temperature of the soda or the size of the raisins that made a difference?

SIZE OF RAISIN	NUMBER OF BOBS		
	Raisin 1	Raisin 2	Raisin 3
Small (currants)	11111	1111	1111
Medium (raisins)	111	11111	1111111
Big (jumbo raisins)	1111	111111	111111

5 Draw a tally chart to record your results. Carry out your test and mark down the number of bobs on the chart. See left for an example of some results (not real ones).

6 What did you find out? As you have counted more than one raisin in each test you have ended up with lots of numbers. Now you need to do some math to work out the mean (average) number of bobs for each size of raisin.

The mean (average) is what you get when you add up all the bobs for one size of raisin and share it out between the raisins —you can use a calculator for this!

SIZE OF RAISIN	NUMBER OF BOBS	MEAN
Small (currants)	5+4+4 = 13	13÷3 = 4.33
Medium (raisins)	3+5+7 = 15	15÷3 = 5
Big (jumbo raisins)	4+6+6 =16	16÷3 = 5.33

7 Now look for a pattern. In this example, the jumbo raisins bobbed more than the raisins which bobbed more than the currants. This means that you could write an ER sentence of your results: "The biggER the raisin, the more times it bobbed" or "The smallER the raisin, the fewER times it bobbed," which says the same thing. Remember your results may not tell you anything. You may have to do the test more times to find a pattern or there may not be a pattern to find. Science is complicated!

8 Finally, *think*. Did your results fit your prediction? If they did, your reasoning may be correct. If they didn't, and they didn't in this example, can you think of a way of explaining what went on? Maybe the bigger raisins had more places for bubbles to form on. It doesn't matter if you are right or wrong. The important thing is to begin thinking scientifically and to have fun doing proper scientific investigations!

a little bit about molecules

Wherever the science is explained in this book you will find words like molecule, polymer, chemical reaction, solid, liquid, or gas. Here's a little bit about what they mean.

Molecules are what most things are made of, including you! They are unbelievably tiny, but they are not the tiniest things scientists have discovered. Molecules are made of atoms, and even atoms are made of smaller parts, including electrons—another word you'll find in this book.

Think about what you have just read. The sentences are made of words, which are made of letters. If everything in the world is like a written language, the atoms are the letters. There are 26 letters in the Latin alphabet (used here), which can be put together into words in billions of different ways. There are about 100 different types of atoms, so they can be put together in even more ways than letters. The different atoms are called elements. You may know the names of many elements already: oxygen, hydrogen, aluminum, iron, gold, silver, copper, chlorine, helium, and carbon are a few of them. These atoms can join up with other atoms to make molecules, just as letters join up to make up words.

Molecules are written down in a code, with letters standing for the atoms. For example:

Water is H_2O = 2 hydrogen (H) atoms + 1 oxygen (O) atom

Carbon dioxide is CO_2 = 1 carbon (C) atom + 2 oxygen (O) atoms

When molecules rearrange themselves or swap atoms with other different molecules to make new substances, it is called a chemical reaction. Sometimes you know chemical reactions are happening because you see bubbles. This is because a gas has been made in the reaction. Molecules come in many different shapes and sizes and have different properties, depending on how their atoms are arranged.

Polymers

Polymers are very big complicated molecules made of many, many special small, repeating, molecular building blocks called monomers, which join together in long chains—like a repeating pattern of beads in a necklace. There can be hundreds of thousands or even millions of monomers in one polymer chain.

Since polymers are so long, things happen to them that don't happen to other molecules—they can get tangled up; they can be curled up and then straighten out; they can stick to each other side by side; and when they move they can only slide over each other very slowly. This makes them really interesting because it affects how the material which they form behaves.

For instance, how stretchy it is, how strong it is, and how much it bounces when you drop it.

Solids, liquids, and gases

Sir Isaac Newton, a very famous scientist who lived in England in the 17th century, worked out the differences between solids, liquids, and gases from

Water molecule H_2O

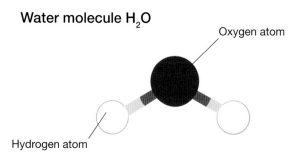

Oxygen atom

Hydrogen atom

the way they behaved. Here are some of the things he said:

Solids

• A solid keeps its shape unless you bang or cut it, or apply some other force to it, in which case it becomes a new shape that it keeps.

• Even though substances made from tiny particles such as sugar, salt, and sand can be poured, they are all solids because each particle keeps the same shape and size. If you pour some salt into a cup, for example, it will make a pile in the center—it doesn't spread out to fill the shape of the cup.

• The molecules in a solid are held together tightly and cannot move. That's why a solid keeps its shape.

Liquids

• A liquid can flow or be poured from one container to another. It will run out of your hand if you try to hold on it.

• A liquid will take the shape of the container into which it is poured. The surface of a liquid always becomes flat and horizontal, although this might take some time for a very viscous (thick) liquid.

• The molecules in a liquid are not as tightly packed together as they are in a solid, and can move and slide past each other. That's why a liquid will take the shape of its container.

Gases

• Solids and liquids can be transparent but are never invisible. Many gases are invisible. Air is a mixture of different invisible gases.

• Gases do not keep their shape and don't always take up the same amount of space. They spread out to fill whatever container they are in and will escape if the container isn't sealed.

• Gas molecules move about freely and have a lot of empty space between them. This means they can be compressed easily (squashed into a smaller space).

FASCINATING FACT
Scientists have found out that atoms can join together in different ways, so we can't say that everything is made of molecules. Some metal atoms, for instance, join together in a lattice or framework, which is not a molecule. The biggest molecule known has over 400,000 atoms.

cool chemistry

color magic

This experiment makes science look like magic! Add a few drops of another liquid to your red cabbage water and watch it instantly change color! The indicator lets you know if a liquid is an acid, an alkali, or in between (neutral). Strong acids are very dangerous but you will find weak ones that are safe to handle—like lemon juice and vinegar—in your kitchen. Acids give foods a sour or "sharp" taste. Alkalis are substances that react with acids and neutralize them. Soap and detergent are alkaline.

SAFETY FIRST
Always ask an adult before using any liquids, especially cleaning liquids.

You will need

½ red cabbage

Kitchen scissors

Medium-sized bowl

Packet of about 10 small transparent plastic cups

Strainer (sieve)

Pitcher (jug)

Lots of different liquids from your kitchen such as lemon juice, white wine vinegar, dishwasher tablet, apple juice, lemonade, baking soda (bicarbonate of soda) (mixed with a little water)—colorless or light-colored liquids are best

Yogurt pots or small cups

Teaspoon or pipette/dropper

Sticky labels

Pencil

1 Pull the layers of the cabbage apart and use the scissors to cut the leaves into small pieces. You don't need the thick stems. Put the pieces into the bowl.

2 Ask an adult to help you boil a kettle and then cover the cabbage with boiling water and leave for about 10 minutes.

3 While the mixture is cooling, line up the plastic cups on a table or work surface and assemble all the different liquids you are going to test. Make sure you ask an adult which ones you can use and be especially careful with any cleaning products—do not use these without an adult's help. You might want to protect the surface to prevent stains.

4 When the cabbage mixture is cool pour it through the strainer (sieve) into the pitcher (jug). The liquid is your indicator—it should be a nice purple color (you can throw away the cooked cabbage).

5 Pour a little cabbage water into each cup so there is about ½ in. (1 cm) of liquid in each cup.

6 Cut a lemon in half and squeeze the juice into a yogurt pot (or use lemon juice from a bottle). Use the pipette/dropper to add a few drops of lemon juice to one cup. What color does it turn? Label the cup *"Lemon juice"* and remember that lemon juice is an acid (see Inside the Science, opposite). Wash the pipette—you will need to wash the pipette each time you use it so that you don't mix up the different liquids.

7 Ask an adult to dissolve part of a dishwasher tablet in some warm water in another pot. (This can hurt your skin so you shouldn't touch it.) With the adult's help, add a few drops of the liquid to the next cup. What color does it turn? Label the cup *"Liquid detergent."* Remember that dishwasher detergent dissolved in water makes a strong alkali.

8 Now pour a little vinegar into another yogurt pot and add a few drops to the next cup. Continue to add different liquids to the cups. Be a good scientist and label each one as you go. You should end up with a range of different color liquids in the cups. Some liquids won't have changed the color of the cabbage water. These liquids are neutral—neither acid nor alkali.

COLOR-CHANGE CABBAGE!

9 Now arrange all the cups on the work surface. Put the acids at one end—these are all shades of red (like the lemon juice). Put the alkalis at the other—these are shades of green and blue (like the dishwasher detergent). Put the neutral ones in the middle; these didn't change the color of the cabbage water. You can tell which are the strongest acids and alkalis by how dramatic the color change is! Put the strongest acid at one end, the strongest alkali at the other, and then try to decide in which order the others will go in order of how strong they are.

INSIDE THE SCIENCE

All liquids have something called a pH value, which tells you about their chemical makeup and how they react with other chemicals. The scale ranges from 0 to 14. A liquid with a pH value between 0 and 7 is acid. A pH value of around 7 is neutral and between 7 and 14 the liquid is an alkali. Acids with very a low pH or alkalis with a very high pH are very strong and very dangerous.

make your own plastic

Look around you and you will discover that a huge number of the things you own and use are made of plastic. You may or may not know that all these plastics are made from oil—the same oil that gasoline (petrol) is made from. Don't worry, we're not using gasoline to make plastic today, we're going to use milk. That's right—milk!

You will need

1 cup (240 ml) whole milk

Measuring cup or pitcher (jug) or small pan

Oven mitt

1 tablespoon white vinegar

Strainer (sieve)

Bowl

Spoon

Paper towels

Cookie cutters or molds for play dough or sugarcraft

1 Ask an adult to help you to heat the milk in a microwave or in a pan on the stovetop. It needs to be hot, but not boiling. Make sure you wear an oven mitt when handling the pitcher (jug) or pan.

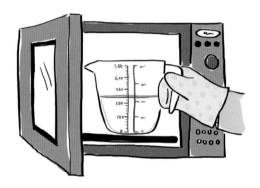

2 Add the vinegar and stir. The milk will "curdle"—this is when solid pieces start to clump together, leaving a clear liquid. Leave it for a few minutes to cool so it is safe to work with.

3 Put the strainer (sieve) over the bowl and pour the milk mixture into it. The solid pieces will be caught in the strainer. Wait for a little while for all the liquid to drain through, then tip the liquid down the sink as you don't need it.

4 Tip the solid white pieces from the strainer into the bowl and work them with the back of a spoon or with your fingers. Keep squishing them together until they become a smooth lump, a bit like a piece of play dough. This is your plastic.

INSIDE THE SCIENCE
The plastic you have made is a simple one called casein. When the curds in the milk react with the vinegar the casein is left in blobs. Casein is a polymer (see page 9) similar to the plastic molecules made from oil. As the casein dries it hardens because the molecules bond together more tightly.

5 Fold up some paper towels into a pad with several layers. Tip the plastic on top and leave it for about 30 minutes so that some of the water that is still in it is soaked up by the paper.

6 Now use your cutters to mold the plastic into different shapes. Leave the shapes to dry out and harden up for a couple of days—near a warm radiator is ideal. You can now paint or decorate your shapes—this is a great way to make Christmas decorations!

MAKE PLASTIC FROM MILK!

basic PVA slime

This is the original PVA-glue slime recipe. Before slime became so popular, this was the slime used in science classes to get kids interested in chemistry because of all the amazing things it can do. Many slimes build on this basic recipe and then add different ingredients.

You will need

½ cup (120 ml) white PVA glue

Medium mixing bowl

Measuring cup or pitcher (jug)

½ cup (120 ml) water

½ teaspoon baking soda (bicarbonate of soda)

Mixing spoon

Food coloring (optional)

About 1 tablespoon slime activator (eyewash or contact lens solution). Must contain boric acid and sodium borate—check the ingredients carefully.

Small cup

Teaspoon or pipette/dropper

Read the slime safety information on page 190.

1 Pour the PVA glue into the bowl and add the water and baking soda (bicarbonate of soda). Stir well until everything is thoroughly mixed together. If you wish, mix in a little food coloring, too.

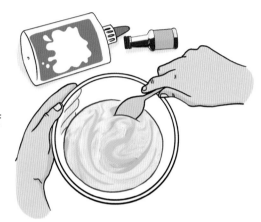

2 Pour the activator into the small cup. Use the teaspoon or a pipette/dropper to add the activator to the glue a little at a time. Keep stirring the mixture as you add the activator. The mixture will gradually get more stringy and start to come away from the sides of the bowl.

3 Continue mixing in the activator, a little at a time, until the slime reaches the consistency you want—the more activator you add, the firmer the slime will be. The more often you make slime, the better you will become at judging how much activator to use.

4 When you think the slime is ready, put a few drops of activator on your hands, then pick it up and start stretching and folding it. The slime might be a bit sticky at first, but will become soft and stretchy, and lose its stickiness, as you work it. Put a little more activator on your hands if the slime is still sticky and keep kneading it until it feels like a good slime.

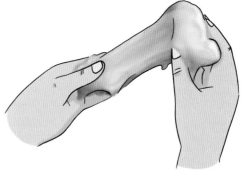

SQUELCH IT, SQUEEZE IT, SQUISH IT!

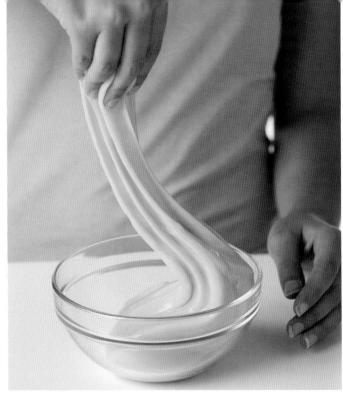

LET'S INVESTIGATE
Make different batches of slime—make some that are firmer and some softer by adding more or less activator. Do they behave in different ways? Try kneading them together into one big lump of slime.

5 Now start exploring what your slime can do and have a go at these experiments:

• How far will the slime stretch? Slowly stretch the slime between your hands until it is as long and thin as you can make it.

• Does the slime bounce? Roll the slime into a ball and see.

• Does the slime flow? Flatten the slime into a pancake and put it on top of an upside-down cup.

• What happens if you tug the slime apart sharply?

• Hold a pancake of slime by its edge— what happens?

• What happens if you put some of the slime in a jelly mold?

INSIDE THE SCIENCE
The polymers (see page 9) in PVA glue can slide over each other fairly easily when the glue is liquid—although it can sometimes seem to take ages for glue to pour from the bottle! Borax activator (see page 190) contains borate ions (charged particles). When you add borax activator to PVA glue, the ions act as "cross-linkers," linking the long polymer molecules together and turning the long strands into a kind of net. But is the resulting slime a solid or a liquid (see pages 9–10)?

When the slime isn't being pushed or pulled, it behaves like a liquid, but when you apply a force—pulling it apart sharply or pressing it together—it behaves like a solid. Imagine the net of molecules all tangled up, but always moving and twisting. Pull on the slime slowly and the molecules have time to become lined up next to each other, so they will slide apart—that's the slime acting like a liquid. But if you tug at the slime sharply, the molecules don't have time to line up. Instead, they end up knotted together more tightly and the slime will act like a solid.

crunchy slime

The best thing about slime is how it feels between your fingers when you squish and squeeze it. Crunchy slime is made by adding little polystyrene balls before the activator. You could also make the slime crunchy by adding snipped-up, plastic drinking straws or little beads.

You will need

1 cup (240 ml) white PVA glue

¼ cup (60 ml) water

1 teaspoon baking soda (bicarbonate of soda)

2–3 cups (480–720 ml) shaving foam

2–3 handfuls of tiny, multicolored polystyrene balls

About 2–3 tablespoons slime activator (eyewash or contact lens solution). Must contain boric acid and sodium borate—check the ingredients carefully.

Large mixing bowl

Measuring cup or pitcher (jug)

Teaspoon

Mixing spoon

Tablespoon

Read the slime safety information on page 190.

SAFETY FIRST
Polystyrene balls are so light that it is possible to breathe them in. Store them carefully in a sealed bag and be sure to keep them away from young children.

1 Add the PVA glue, water, and baking soda (bicarbonate of soda) to the bowl and stir until everything is thoroughly mixed together.

2 Squirt in the shaving foam and add the polystyrene balls, then mix everything together really well.

3 Add 1 tablespoon of activator to the mixture and start stirring. When the mixture becomes gloopy and starts coming together, use your hands to stretch, fold, and pull it for 5 minutes—it will be very sticky to start with.

4 Add another ½ tablespoon of activator and keep stirring—the mixture will transform into a stretchy, crunchy slime. Add more activator, a teaspoon at a time, if the slime still feels sticky. Remember to add the activator in tiny amounts—if you add too much, your slime may be too stiff to play with.

TOP TIP

Polystyrene is a polymer (see page 9) that does not biodegrade and cannot be recycled, making it bad for the environment. We've included this project because of the interesting science behind it, but you may want to use a non-plastic alternative to add crunch—something that isn't plastic and yet won't absorb water from the slime! Try experimenting (jumbo oats work quite well), but remember food products will go bad, so if you add any, keep the slime in the fridge and throw it away after a day or two.

LET'S INVESTIGATE
Does adding polystyrene balls make the slime break more easily? What happens when you stretch the slime thinly or let it run down the sides of an upturned bowl? If you leave the slime overnight in a Ziplock bag, what happens? Predict whether the balls will end up at the top or bottom of the slime.

INSIDE THE SCIENCE

The colorful balls in this slime are made from a material called polystyrene. This is another kind of polymer—a long molecule with a repeating pattern (see page 9). Polystyrene is incredibly light because it is made up of a net of molecules that are puffed full of air, whereas slime is made of a similar net of molecules that is full of water, which means it is much heavier.

You could also compare polystyrene to shaving foam. Polystyrene is mostly air bubbles contained by a solid, whereas shaving foam is mostly air bubbles contained by a liquid. The polystyrene balls rise to the surface of the slime if you leave it overnight because they float on the liquid slime as they would in water.

glowing lava lamp

You'll soon be hypnotized watching the bubbles rise through the oil in this beautiful lava lamp. If you make your lamp after dark, drop in a glow stick, switch off the lights, and you will have an even more magical experience.

You will need

Glass tumbler

Vegetable oil (you will need quite a lot)

Teaspoon

Funnel

Water

Clear plastic bottle

Food coloring

Alka-Seltzer tablets (or fizzing Vitamin C tablets)

Glow stick (optional)

1 Before you start making your lava lamp, have a bit of fun investigating oil and water. Fill a glass with water and then drop in a teaspoon of oil. Watch what happens to the oil. Stir it hard to mix it into the water and then wait and watch!

2 Now to make your lamp. Using the funnel, pour water into the bottle until it is about a quarter full.

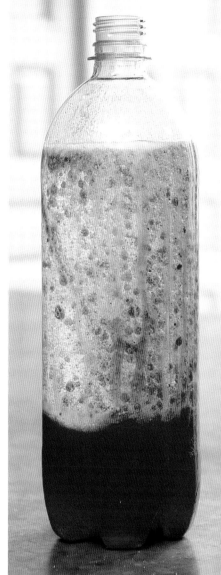

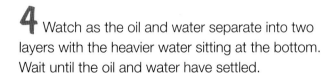

3 Using the funnel again, pour in the vegetable oil until the bottle is a bit more than three-quarters full. You need to leave room for your glow stick.

4 Watch as the oil and water separate into two layers with the heavier water sitting at the bottom. Wait until the oil and water have settled.

LET YOURSELF BE MESMERIZED...

5 Add about 12 drops of food coloring. Watch as it falls through the oil—the coloring will not mix with the oil. It will fall until it meets the water and will then sit on top of the water for a few seconds before bursting into the water and then spreading out. Gently twist the bottle a few times to help the color mix with the water, but don't stir or shake it.

6 Now, break an Alka-Seltzer (or fizzing Vitamin C) tablet into about 4 smaller pieces. Drop one piece of the tablet into the bottle. It will drop through the oil into the water and begin to fizz. Watch as bubbles begin to erupt through the oil. When the bubbling begins to slow down, add another piece of Alka-Seltzer and it will start all over again.

7 For the full glow show, bend your glow stick to activate it, drop it into the bottle, and switch off the lights.

INSIDE THE SCIENCE

Oil and water don't mix. The less dense oil floats on top of water (less dense means the same amount is less heavy). When you drop the piece of Alka-Seltzer into the lava lamp bottle it drops through the oil and into the water and reacts with the water, fizzing and releasing small bubbles of carbon dioxide. These bubbles get attached to blobs of water and act like floats. The blobs rise up to the surface through the oil. When they reach the surface, the gas escapes and without its float to hold it up, the more dense water sinks back down.

creeping colors

What color is the ink in your black marker pen? Did you say black? Think again! Using filter paper, watch as water creeps through different inks and spreads them out into amazing strips of different colors. This is called chromatography and it lets you find out just what different colors make up the inks you use. Try this experiment using several glasses and pencils so you can work on lots of different color inks at the same time.

You will need

Coffee filter papers (white ones, not unbleached brown ones)

Scissors

Glass tumbler or clear plastic cup

Sticky tape

Pencil

Pack of colored marker pens

1 Cut several long strips of coffee filter paper about ½ in. (1 cm) wide and just longer than the height of the glass.

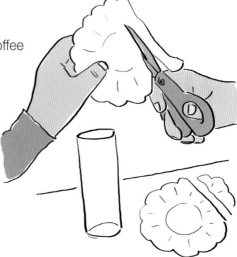

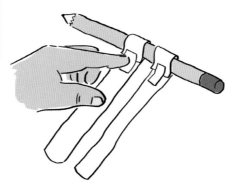

2 Tape each strip to the middle of a pencil. You can probably tape two, or even three, strips to each pencil if the strips are narrow and your glass quite wide.

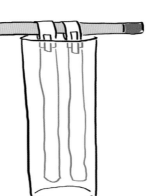

3 Place the pencil over the top of the glass with the paper strips dangling down inside. Check that the ends hang just above the bottom of the glass.

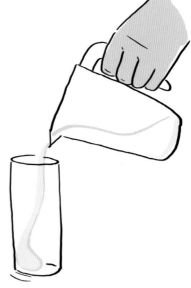

4 Take away the pencil while you pour enough water into the glass so that the bottom of the paper strips will just reach it.

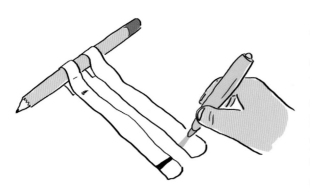

5 Using a different colored marker pen for each strip, draw a line across the bottom of each paper strip, about 1 in. (2.5 cm) from the bottom. Let it dry and then draw another line, using the same color, over the top of the first. Do this a couple of times so you have plenty of ink on your paper. In pencil, at the top of the strip, write what color you have used on that strip (it will be surprisingly difficult to tell later on).

HOW MANY COLORS MAKE BLACK?

6 Place the pencil back over the glass. The ends of the strips should just hang in the water but the ink line must be above the water.

7 Wait and watch as the water creeps up the paper, carrying the ink with it and separating it out into different colors. Which color markers only have one color ink in them? Which are made up of lots of colors? Which has the most colors?

INSIDE THE SCIENCE

Some inks are made up of more than one color. The molecules of the chemicals that make these colors have different "likes." Some are attracted to water more than paper and some are attracted to paper more than water. The ones that are most attracted to water are carried along with it quickly as it travels up the paper. The ones that are attracted to paper stick to the paper and don't move much, if at all.

rainbow in a glass

Normally, if you added water that has been colored with different food colorings to a glass, the colors would mix together. For example, if you mixed yellow and blue water you would get green. In this project you slowly add different colored waters to a glass and end up with a beautiful rainbow of different layers of color!

You will need

4 plastic cups

Teaspoon

Sugar

Measuring cup or pitcher (jug)

Spoon for mixing

Blue, red, green, and yellow food coloring

Glass tumbler

Plastic medicine syringe

1 Line up the four plastic cups and add sugar to them as follows:
Cup 1—1 teaspoon
Cup 2—2 teaspoons
Cup 3—3 teaspoons
Cup 4—4 teaspoons

2 Add ¼ cup (60 ml) of hot water from the faucet (tap) to each of the cups and then stir each one until all the sugar has dissolved. (If the sugar won't dissolve ask an adult to help you to put the cups into the microwave, heat them for 30 seconds, and then stir again).

3 Add blue food coloring to cup 1, red to cup 2, green to cup 3, and yellow to cup 4. Stir each cup again. (Wash the spoon between stirs!)

INSIDE THE SCIENCE

When sugar is dissolved in water, the water becomes more dense. (Dense means heavier for the same amount of water.) The more sugar you add, the more dense the water will be. In the glass, the heavier (more dense) yellow water stays at the bottom and the less dense waters float in layers above it. The lightest (least dense) blue water floats on the top.

4 Pour the yellow water into the glass tumbler.

5 Fill the plastic syringe with green water. Hold the tip of the syringe just above the surface of the yellow water and, very slowly and carefully press the plunger so that the green water dribbles down over the yellow. You may have to fill the syringe several times depending on the size of your syringe. Do the same with the red water next, and finally the blue. The four different colors will stay in separate layers to make a rainbow!

MAKE A LIQUID RAINBOW!

pop-up glove

Question: How do you get the air holes in bread, which make it look like sponge?

Answer: By using yeast. Yeast is a microorganism (a living thing that is too small to be seen with the naked eye). When we mix it with flour, sugar, water, and salt to make bread it feeds off the sugar and produces the gas carbon dioxide. This is what makes bubbles in the bread dough. But yeast is a bit like Goldilocks in the story of the Three Bears. It doesn't like things too hot or too cold; they need to be just right. You can see this by watching the gloves in this experiment. If the yeast produces carbon dioxide gas it will inflate the glove to make a pop-up hand on top of the cup!

You will need

3 small transparent plastic cups (the gloves should fit tightly over the top of the cups)

3 sticky labels

Active dried yeast (for baking)

Measuring teaspoon (5 ml)

Sugar

Water

Measuring cup or pitcher (jug)

Spoon for stirring

Waterproof tray

3 latex gloves (the type doctors use)

1 Label the cups 1, 2, and 3.

2 Put one teaspoon of dried yeast into each cup. Each teaspoon of dried yeast contains millions of microscopic yeast cells!

3 Add two teaspoons of sugar to each cup.

4 Ask an adult to boil some water in a kettle and then let it cool for about 5 minutes so that it is still quite hot, but not boiling.

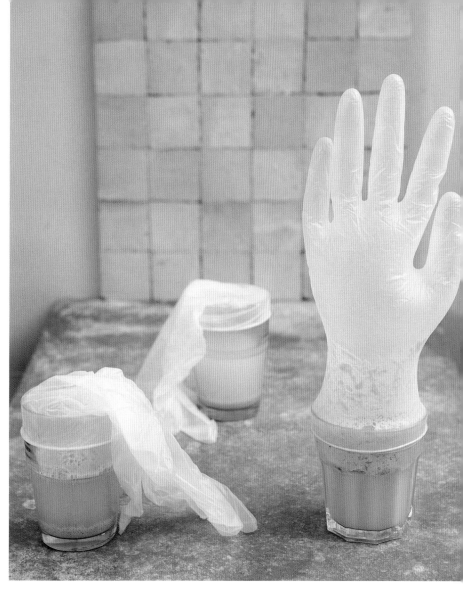

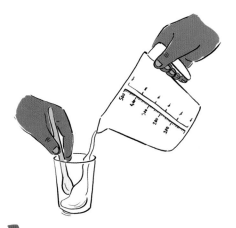

5 Measure ½ cup (100 ml) of cold water into the measuring cup or pitcher (jug), pour it into cup 1, and stir it well.

6 Now measure about ⅓ cup (70 ml) of cold water into the cup or pitcher and then very carefully add hot water until you have ½ cup (100 ml). The water should be cool enough to put your finger into comfortably. Pour this into cup 2 and stir well.

WATCH THE GHOSTLY HAND RISE UP!

7 Lastly, very carefully measure ½ cup (100 ml) of hot water and pour it into cup 3. Stir it well.

8 Making sure that you don't spill the mixture, carefully put a glove over the top of each cup. Stand the cups together on a tray.

9 Now you need to wait. Watch carefully to see if you can see any bubbles forming in the mixtures or any froth on the top. Froth will show that the yeast is feeding on the sugar and making bubbles of carbon dioxide. Keep checking every 10 minutes to see what is happening. You could leave the experiment for several hours or even overnight. Which of the gloves do you think will pop up? What do you think might happen to the yeast in cup 3 with the very hot water? What do you think will happen with the cold water?

INSIDE THE SCIENCE

The water activates the dried yeast, bringing it back to life (because all living things need water). The yeast then feeds on the sugar and, as a waste product, produces carbon dioxide, which inflates the glove. Because yeast is living it needs to be at a certain temperature to be properly alive and active. The best temperature for activating yeast is 105–115°F (41–46°C). Very hot water will kill the yeast.

balloon fire extinguisher

If you don't like balloons bursting this probably isn't the best project for you—but it's fun and interesting. Have you heard of the fire triangle? The fire triangle tells you that you need three things for a fire to burn—fuel, heat, and oxygen. Take away any of those and the fire will go out. In this project you can try putting out a candle using three different balloon fire extinguishers, but you will need an adult's help for this.

You will need

Balloon pump

3 similar-sized balloons but in different colors, ideally white, blue, and yellow

Teaspoon

Baking soda (bicarbonate of soda)

Small plastic bottle—the balloon neck must be able to fit over the top of the bottle

Funnel

Tablespoon

White household vinegar

Water

Votive candle (tealight)

Second timer

1 Use the pump to inflate each of the balloons a few times so that they are well stretched.

2 Put 3 teaspoons of baking soda (bicarbonate of soda) into the bottle. Now use the funnel to pour about 2 tablespoons of vinegar into the yellow balloon (you may need some help with this!).

3 Taking care not to spill the vinegar, stretch the neck of the yellow balloon over the top of the bottle.

4 Now hold the balloon up so that the vinegar spills into the bottle. The vinegar and baking soda will react to produce a foam of carbon dioxide gas, which will inflate the balloon. If it doesn't inflate that much, twist the neck of the balloon so no carbon dioxide escapes (you'll need a helper at this point), add some more baking soda and vinegar to the bottle, and then reattach the balloon. When it is well inflated tie a knot in the neck.

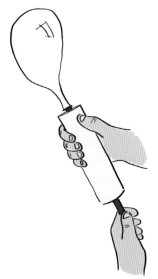

5 Now inflate the white balloon, using the pump, until it is about the same size as the yellow balloon and tie a knot in the neck.

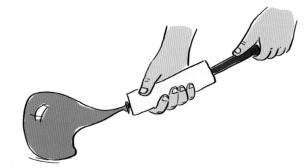

6 Wash out the funnel and use it to pour some water into the blue balloon. Now use the pump to inflate it until it is the same size as the white and yellow ones. You now have three balloon fire extinguishers—which do you think will put out a fire?

7 You will need an adult's help for the testing stage. Ask an adult to light a votive candle (tealight). If you are feeling brave, hold the white, air-filled balloon just above the candle (NOT in the flame) for just 15 seconds or until the balloon bursts—whichever is quicker. You may want to ask an adult to do this while you cover your ears! What happens to the balloon and the flame?

WHICH ONE WILL WORK?

8 Next, try with the blue, water-filled balloon. Hold it above the flame for just 15 seconds, no longer, or until it bursts—whichever is quicker. What happens to the balloon and flame?

9 Finally, use the yellow carbon dioxide filled balloon for just 15 seconds or until it bursts. What happens to the balloon and flame this time? Which was the best fire extinguisher?

INSIDE THE SCIENCE

The air from the white balloon does not put out the flame because it just gives it more oxygen. The blue balloon won't have burst at all—the water takes away the heat from the candle so the rubber doesn't melt and burst. The yellow balloon extinguishes the flame because carbon dioxide gas is heavier than air so when the balloon bursts the gas sinks down over the flame and drives away all the oxygen. Many real fire extinguishers are filled with carbon dioxide for this reason— you will probably see them around your school, in restaurants, and other public places.

delicious fizz

Have you ever bitten into a sherbet lemon candy and felt a cold fizz on your tongue? The fizz and the coldness are chemistry happening in your mouth! Usually in science we say, "Never put anything in your mouth!" but this is an exception. It's a quick and very tasty project.

You will need

Small bowl or cup

Measuring spoon

Measuring cup

¼ cup (30 g) confectioner's (icing) sugar

½ teaspoon citric acid

½ teaspoon baking soda (bicarbonate of soda)

Spoon for mixing

1 Mix together all the dry ingredients in the bowl.

2 Taste the mixture and feel what is happening! Enjoy!

INSIDE THE SCIENCE

Here you have an acid (citric acid) mixing with an alkali (baking soda) (see page 15). While they are both dry they don't react. As soon as you put them in your mouth, saliva mixes with them and they begin to react and produce carbon dioxide—that's the fizz! The coldness is because this reaction takes heat from its surroundings—in this case, your tongue so it feels strangely, but nicely, cold. The sugar doesn't cause any reaction at all— it just tastes nice!

bubble colors

In this project we'll think about the color of bubbles. One reason everyone loves bubbles is because they are so delicate, shimmery, and beautiful, but have you looked at a bubble really closely to see what makes it so special?

You will need

Bubble mix (see page 4)

Simple round bubble wand

Transparent plastic lid (from a yogurt pot or potato chip tube)

Sticky tape

Flashlight (torch)

Spoon

Drinking straw or pipette bubble wand

1 Start outside in the daylight. Blow some bubbles using a simple round bubble wand and catch one back onto your wand. Look for two reflections—one the right way up and the other upside down. Watch closely for swirling colors, too.

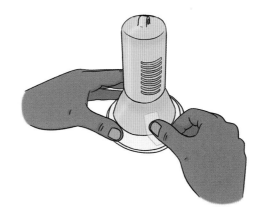

2 Now go into a dark room (with the light on at first). Tape the plastic lid onto the front of the flashlight (torch), with the rim up, like a shallow bowl. Hold the flashlight upright with the lid on top.

3 Use your finger to wet the plastic lid with bubble mix, including around the rim, and then put a spoonful of mix into the lid. Use the straw or pipette bubble wand to blow one big bubble dome to cover the lid.

4 Turn the lights off and the flashlight on. Hold the flashlight with the bubble in front of your face and look up into the bubble. Can you see all the colors of the rainbow? Perhaps not all of them and, if you watch very closely, the colors you see may change before the bubble pops. What patterns of color do you see?

5 Now dip the straw or pipette wand in bubble mix, push it inside the bubble, and blow gently—watch as the colors change and swirl around.

LET'S INVESTIGATE
Try to record which colors you can see and how they change—using a voice recorder might be the easiest way. Experiment with different-colored cellophane under the transparent lid. What does this do to the colors? Also, try different light sources. Do LED flashlights give you different colors than old-fashioned filament flashlights?

INSIDE THE SCIENCE

Find a shiny spoon and look into it; your reflection is upside down. Turn it over and look at the back; your reflection is the right way up. A mirror that curves in (concave) gives an upside-down reflection. The inside of the bubble is curved in like this. Light passes through the transparent (see-through) outside of the bubble and reflects off the inside surface on the opposite side—this makes an upside-down reflection. But some light also reflects off the bubble's outside surface, which curves out (convex), and this gives a reflection that is the right way up, like the one on the back of your spoon.

All the different colors you see in the bubble are because light is made up of all the colors of the rainbow. Each color has a different wavelength. The bubble film is a sandwich of water molecules between dish soap molecules.

When white light hits the soap film, some reflects off the outer layer of soap molecules and some off the inner layer a tiny distance away. This means that the wavelengths of the different colors in the two reflections are slightly out of step, as one had further to travel, and so they "interfere." Some waves cancel each other out; some get together and are stronger—these are the colors you can see.

As water evaporates from the bubble, the space between the two layers gets thinner so that some wavelengths interfere and you see different colors. When they are about to pop, they look black. Moving air also changes the thickness.

bubbles inside bubbles

If you touch a bubble, it will pop—true? False! You can push things right inside bubbles and they won't burst. This is what you're going to do in this activity: It takes a bit of skill and patience but has amazing results.

You will need

Smooth surface, such as a kitchen counter top or a plastic tray

Bubble mix (see page 4)

Pipette bubble wand (made from cutting the top of the bulb off a plastic pipette)

Drinking straw

1 Clean your smooth surface with some of your bubble mix; make sure there are no dips, bumps, grease spots, or crumbs. Now spread a circle of bubble mix on the surface with your fingers.

2 Use the pipette bubble wand to blow a large half bubble (hemisphere) onto the wet circle. A straw will work if you don't have a pipette wand, but it will be harder to blow big bubbles.

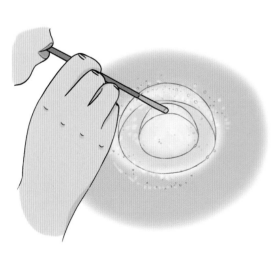

3 Dip the straw into the bubble mix—you could use the pipette again but the straw may work better. Carefully push the straw through the first bubble (if the straw is wet with bubble mix, the first bubble shouldn't burst), and slowly blow another bubble. Watch what happens to the first bubble as you blow.

INSIDE THE SCIENCE

Anything dry is a bubble's arch enemy! Imagine two friends holding your hands and pulling you in opposite directions. You will stay still. If one lets go, you'll be pulled straight into the other friend. Water molecules in bubbles are being pulled from both sides. When the bubble lands on a dry surface, there are no water molecules pulling from the dry side so the edge of the bubble is pulled away from the surface toward the center and it bursts. The bubble doesn't pop on the wet counter top or with the wet pipette because the molecules still have "friends" on both sides!

4 Repeat the process, pushing your straw through the two bubbles before you blow the next. Keep going!

LET'S INVESTIGATE

How many bubbles within bubbles can you make? What happens to the outside bubble each time you add another bubble? Try wetting a long nail or needle with bubble mix and pushing it right through the bubble. Can you do the same with your finger?

bubble tennis

Have you ever tried to catch a bubble? The chances are that as soon as you touched one it popped. Here is a clever way of catching a bubble and seeing it bounce. Why not play bubble tennis, bouncing it to a friend?
You could add multiple players and make up your own bubble game.

You will need

Pair of clean knitted gloves (one glove for each player)

Bubble mix (see page 4)

Bubble wand

1 Each player puts a knitted glove on one hand. Blow a few bubbles and hold out your gloved hand to catch one. It won't pop, it will bounce.

2 Bounce it on to a friend to play bubble tennis, or simply bounce it from hand to hand. How many pats can you give it before it bursts?

LET'S INVESTIGATE
Experiment with different types of gloves—try latex, cotton, wool, or leather—then try different bubble mixes: remember the bubble only lasts until the water in it evaporates, so mixes that slow down evaporation will work best (see opposite).

INSIDE THE SCIENCE
Grease, oil, and dirt are all bubble busters!
The water molecules in a bubble hate grease and pull away from it,
bursting the bubble. Our hands are naturally slightly oily, so if a bubble
touches your skin it bursts. Gloves provide a barrier between the bubble
and your skin. Bubbles also pop when water evaporates from them.
The glycerin in the bubble mix slows down evaporation so the
bubbles last longer for your game.

bubble prints

This is a very simple activity that combines art, science, and math. The delicate bubble prints are a beautiful way of decorating card or paper for greeting cards or thank-you notes, and while you are about it do a little investigating. There are two different techniques to try here. Which one gives you the best results?

You will need

Food coloring or acrylic (poster) paint

A few shallow bowls

Dish soap (washing-up liquid)

Tablespoon

Drinking straw

Paper—strong absorbent paper or cardstock works best

Pipette bubble wand (made from cutting the top of the bulb off a plastic pipette) (optional)

Scissors

Transparent document wallet

1 Place a squirt of food coloring or paint into a bowl. Add a tablespoon of dish soap (washing-up liquid) and a little water. Mix together well.

2 Use the straw to blow into the paint mix until you have a good mound of colored bubbles in lots of sizes.

3 Hold the paper flat over the bubbles, gently touch the paper on the bubbles, and lift it straight off again. Examine your print. Keep experimenting with the amount of paint, water, and bubble mix to get the clearest prints. You can build up layers of different colors using different bowls for each color. Look carefully at the shapes of the bubble prints you have captured. Are they round?

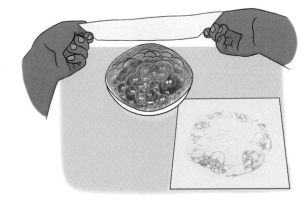

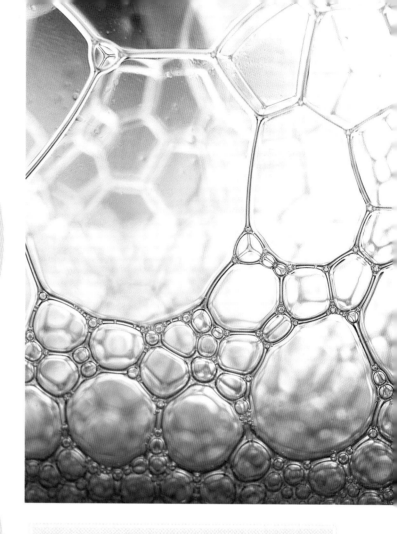

LET'S INVESTIGATE
Cut the top off the document wallet about halfway down, so that the pocket you have left is a bit shorter than a straw. Pour a little bubble mix into the wallet and use a straw to blow bubbles until they rise up into the wallet. Now examine the different shapes you can see.

Another technique is to start with just bubble mix in a clean bowl. Blow a good mound of bubbles and use the pipette to drop a little food coloring on top. Use different colors in different places. The color will collect around the edges of the bubbles. Lay a sheet of paper on top and lift it up to reveal your multicolored print.

INSIDE THE SCIENCE
When two bubbles meet, they join so that they share the wall between them. If the bubbles are the same size, the wall will be flat. Smaller bubbles are at higher pressure than larger ones, so a small bubble will bulge into a bigger one. Where three bubbles join, the angle between the walls will always be 120 degrees. This is the angle inside a regular hexagon. Look at the bubble prints or the bubbles sandwiched in the plastic wallet, and you will see that some of the bubbles form a pattern a bit like a beehive, with hexagon-shaped faces. It is a very efficient shape.

square bubbles

Bubbles are always spheres, except now we're going to show you how to make a square-shaped, or rather a cube-shaped, bubble!

You will need

6 drinking straws

6–9 chenille stems (pipe cleaners)

Scissors

Lots of bubble mix

Large, deep container for the bubble mix—at least 3 in. (7 cm) across and 3 in. (7 cm) deep

Pipette bubble wand (made from cutting the top of the bulb off a plastic pipette)

1 First, make a cube with the straws and chenille stems (pipe cleaners). Cut the straight parts of the straws into 3-in. (7-cm) lengths (throw any bendy parts away); you need 12 pieces. Cut the chenille stems into 4-in. (10-cm) lengths; you also need 12 of these.

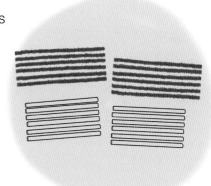

2 Push a chenille stem piece into each straw. Slide the straw to the center and bend up the ends of the chenille stem so the straw stays in place.

3 Hold two straws side by side and twist the chenille stems together. Pull the straws to make a right-angle corner. Stand a third straw upright at the corner and twist the protruding stem from this around the join. Put this to one side and take three more straws and do the same again. Do it twice more so you have four pieces each with three arms—the corners of your cube.

INSIDE THE SCIENCE

Bubbles are usually perfect spheres. What happens in this experiment is that the soap film clings to the sides of the cube, pulling at the bubble. These soap films use the shortest possible distance while still connecting all the sides, which pulls the sphere into a cube. But the bubble is still trying to be a sphere so the sides are bulging.

4 Now twist two ends of two 3D corners together, and add the remaining 3D corners to connect the sides of your cube.

BUBBLES DON'T HAVE TO BE ROUND!

5 Fill your container with bubble mix and dip the cube into it so that it goes right under. Pull it out by one corner. As you pull it out you will see bubble films stretched between the edges of the cube. Give it a little shake and you will see them link together. A square window of bubble film will appear in the center. Shake it around a little and it will change from vertical to horizontal or horizontal to vertical.

6 Put the cube on a flat surface with the square window horizontal. Take the pipette bubble wand and blow a bubble. Shake it so the bubble falls onto the square window. Shake the cube gently and your round bubble will join with the square window to make a cube-shaped bubble (with slightly curved faces). This may take a bit of practice!

7 Try making the bubble bigger. Take the bubble wand and dip it into the bubble mix so it is wet all over the bulb. Slowly push it into the cube-shaped bubble and blow.

LET'S INVESTIGATE
Make some different 3D shapes with straws and chenille stems to blow different-shaped bubbles— for example, you could try a triangular pyramid.

CHAPTER TWO
fab physics

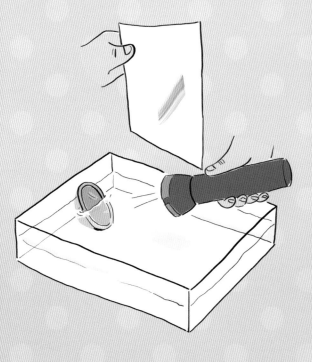

potato pop gun

How about a bit of target practice? For this simple project your only ammunition will be a potato—or maybe two or three because you will find it's so much fun you will want to keep going. Just make sure that the potatoes you use are not needed for your dinner! This is a project you should definitely do in a big outside space, and, most importantly, NEVER fire your pop gun toward a person or animal.

You will need

Length of copper pipe, about 24 in. (60 cm) long

Metal nail file

Colored chalks to draw a target

A few large potatoes

Water-soluble ink or paint and a small pot (optional)

A length of dowel (round wood) or garden cane that fits into the pipe and is about the same length as the pipe

1 You can buy copper pipe cut to length or ask an adult to help you saw a piece. Be careful that the pipe doesn't get bent or dented as you saw—the tube needs to be completely straight and smooth. Use the metal nail file to file away any rough edges from the ends.

2 Find a place to draw a target— maybe a fence or a tree. You need a good length of backyard—about 4 or 5 yards (meters) to fire along. Draw the target like an archery target with different rings for different scores, with the bullseye in the center scoring the highest number of points!

WHO CAN SCORE A BULLSEYE?

3 Put the potato on a firm surface—the ground will do fine. Hold it still and push one end of the tube right through the potato. This will make a plug of potato in the tube. Make sure that the potato completely fills the end of the tube.

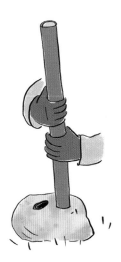

4 Turn the tube over and do the same with the other end so that both ends are plugged with potato.

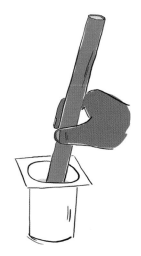

5 If you want your potato to make a mark when it hits the target, pour a little ink or paint into a pot and dip one end of the tube into it.

6 To fire your spud gun you need to poke the piece of dowel or garden cane into the other end of the tube. To do this in one go can be a bit tricky so first push the stick a little way into the tube, pushing the potato in by about ½ in. (1 cm) so that the stick can't slip sideways. Then rest the tube on a table or back of a chair so you can hold it steady. Make sure that there is no one in the way, take aim, and poke hard! The inky potato plug will shoot out with a pop—and maybe even a puff of smoke! It should make a splat of ink on the target (if you hit it).

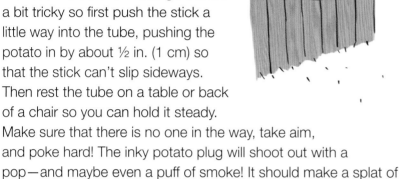

7 Before you go again, clear the tube. Push out the piece of potato that is still in the tube by using your poking stick. It should come out with a pop. Load up with more potato and try again. How accurate can you get?

INSIDE THE SCIENCE

The pieces of potato jammed into each end of the pipe are so tight that no air can get in or out. When the potato at the back is pushed in with the dowel, the space between the two plugs of potato becomes smaller, squeezing the air inside which means the pressure builds up. In the end the pressure is so great that it forces the potato out of the front of the tube.

diver in a bottle

All divers want to sink to the bottom of the ocean so that they can see the fish or explore old wrecks. You can send this pen cap diver to the bottom of the bottle just by squeezing the bottle. It floats to the top again when you let go.

You will need

Glass tumbler

Water

Some modeling clay

Ballpoint pen top—without a hole at the end (the best ones are ones with long side spikes)

2-quart (2-liter) clear plastic bottle

1 Fill the glass with water. Put a blob of modeling clay on the long spike of the pen top and drop it into the water. You want the pen top to just float so that it is hanging straight down in the water with the tip at the surface. Add or take away clay until you have it just right. (If you haven't got this type of pen top, make a ring of clay all around the end of the cap so that it is balanced and floats vertically in the water.)

TRY THIS
To make your diver more realistic, cut out a small diver figure (about the same size as the pen top) from a piece of foil tray. Attach him to the cap with a small paper clip. Test how the cap floats in the glass before you put him in the bottle, adding or taking away clay if you need to.

INSIDE THE SCIENCE
Squeezing the bottle forces the water into the pen cap squashing the bubble of air inside. This means that the diver is more dense, or heavier than the water, and it sinks. When the bottle is released, the air expands again pushing the water out of the pen cap. This means the diver is less dense (lighter) so it floats back to the top.

2 It's best to do this part in the sink! Fill the bottle right to the very top and then drop in the "diver." The water should be level with the top of the plastic. Screw on the lid.

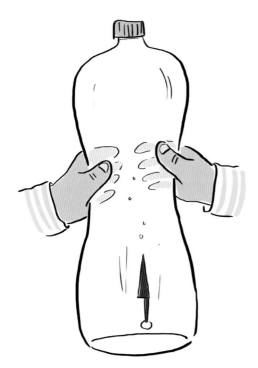

3 Gently squeeze the bottle. The pen cap diver will immediately drop to the bottom of the bottle. Let go and it will float back up again.

WATCH IT RISE AND FALL!

there and back roller

Roll the can along the floor—it stops and then, just like magic, rolls back to where it started. It's all to do with stored energy!

You will need

Hammer

Nail

Board

Empty can with a plastic or metal fitted lid (coffee or cocoa cans are good)

Lots of elastic bands (or a long piece of elastic)

Plastic bag

Scissors

Small weight

Thin string

1 You will need to ask an adult to help you with this step. Use the hammer, nail, and board to punch two holes about 1 in. (2.5 cm) apart in the bottom of the can and two more in the lid. (Watch your fingers when you do this and watch for sharp edges around the holes when you punch through metal.) The holes should be big enough to thread a piece of elastic or an elastic band through.

2 Link the elastic bands together to make one long chain as follows: put one band half on top of another. Bring the end of the bottom band up through the top band and thread the other end of the bottom band through the loop you have made. Pull it tight and link the next band in the same way (or you can use one long piece of elastic).

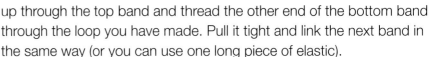

3 Make a little bag for your weight. Cut a square of plastic bag, put the weight on top, gather the plastic up around it, and tie it tightly with some thin string. Make a small loop of string at the top.

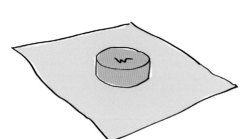

4 Thread the two ends of the elastic band chain/elastic through the two holes at the bottom of the can.

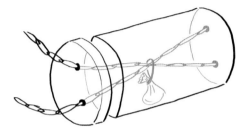

5 Inside the can, thread the weight onto the elastic band chain/elastic. Cross the two ends of the elastic band chain/elastic and thread them through the holes in the lid.

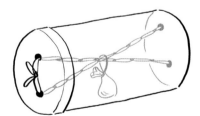

6 Now put the lid on the can and then pull through the ends of the elastic band chain/elastic and tie them together with a knot. The elastic band chain/elastic shouldn't be loose in the can but it shouldn't be too stretched either.

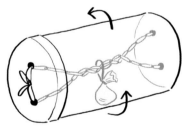

7 Roll the can away from you and wait for it to come rolling back!

OFF IT GOES – BACK IT COMES!

two-ball bounce

Surprise your friends with this very simple trick. It is all to do with the transfer of momentum but what happens is quite unexpected. It's best to do this one outside where nothing can get broken!

You will need

Soccer ball
or basketball

Small ball such as a tennis
ball or a light rubber ball

1 Hold the two balls, one in each hand, at shoulder height. Drop them at the same time and notice how high each one bounces.

2 Pick the balls up. Hold the large ball in one hand. Place the small ball on top and hold it still with the other hand. Again, hold them out at shoulder height.

HOW DID THAT HAPPEN?

3 Let go of both balls together and watch what happens to the small ball!

INSIDE THE SCIENCE

The large ball bounces on the ground first and begins to move upward. It hits the smaller ball, which is still coming down and transfers its momentum to the smaller ball, which then shoots high into the air. How much momentum an object has depends on its speed and how heavy it is. The bigger ball has lots of momentum to transfer to the small ball because it is heavy. If you tried this with a big, but very light, inflatable beach ball as the bottom ball, would it work? Try it!

switch tricks

Hook up the circuits and see your friends jump! You simply set up a buzzer circuit and attach it to different switches. The first switch will set off the buzzer when someone closes the bathroom door. The second sets off the buzzer when someone steps on a mat. The third triggers the buzzer with a tilt switch in a cookie tin.

You will need

To make a circuit, wires, battery pack, batteries, and buzzer. Available online at www.miniscience.com or www.tts-group.co.uk

Cardboard

Scissors

Large paper clips

Sticky tape

Small sponge

Cardboard candy tube, or other small tube with one cardboard end

Small sharp scissors and cutting board

Brads (paper fasteners)

Large metal ball bearing (or a medium-sized marble and some aluminum foil)

Rectangular tin or box with a lid

Paper and pen

BATHROOM DOOR SWITCH

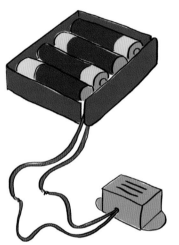

1 First set up a simple circuit with wires, a battery pack and a buzzer. If your circuit does not work turn the buzzer around so that it is connected the other way around —buzzers only work one way in a circuit. Once it works, disconnect it so that you don't run down the batteries.

2 To make the switch for the bathroom door, first cut a rectangle of cardboard about 3½ x 2 in. (9 x 5 cm). Fold it in the middle, bringing short end to meet short end.

SURPRISE YOUR FRIENDS!

3 Push a paper clip onto each short end of the cardboard. Attach a long wire to each of the paper clips.

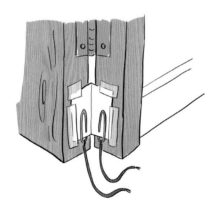

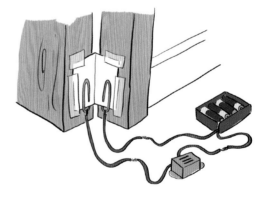

4 With the bathroom door open, use sticky tape to fix the switch below the inside bottom door hinge, so the switch is like a hinge, with half on the door and half on the frame. When the door closes the two halves of cardboard will close together and the two paper clips should touch each other. Be careful no one closes the door while you are setting up your switch—you don't want your fingers to get trapped.

5 Join the wires from the paper clips to the wires of your circuit to make one big circuit. Test it works. When you close the door the paper clips will touch and complete the circuit and the buzzer will buzz loudly! Try to hide the battery and buzzer so that whoever next uses the bathroom doesn't see it!

UNDER THE MAT SWITCH

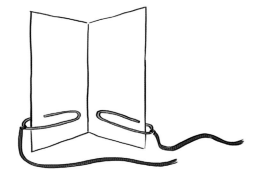

1 Follow steps 1–3 of the instructions for the bathroom door switch but this time push the paper clips across the cardboard, so they cover the width of the cardboard.

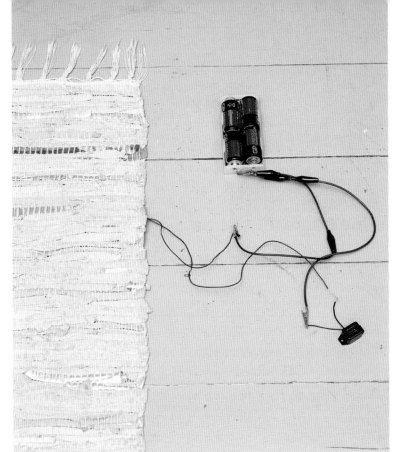

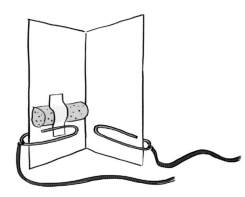

2 Cut a strip of sponge (see left), which is about as long as the paper clips. Tape the sponge just beside one of the paper clips, on the side nearest to the fold. It might be easiest to take off the paper clip while you tape it on and then put it back. The sponge should stop the paper clips touching when you close the cardboard gently.

3 Put the switch under a mat in the place where you think someone is most likely to step. Attach the wires to the buzzer circuit nearby—try to hide it. When someone steps on the mat the sponge will squash flat, the paper clips will touch, and the buzzer will buzz loudly. Step off the mat and the sponge will spring back up and the buzzer will stop.

COOKIE TIN TILT SWITCH

1 Gently open the cardboard end of the candy tube. Bend it back flat and carefully make two small holes about ½ in. (1 cm) apart in the cardboard, using the end of a sharp pair of scissors and pushing down onto a cutting board.

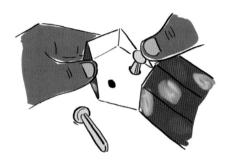

2 Push a brad (paper fastener) through each of the holes from the inside out. They should be side by side but not touching.

3 The diameter (distance across) of the ball bearing or marble you use should be a bit smaller than the width of the tube. If you are using a ball bearing, drop that into the tube. It must be big enough that when it rolls down the tube it will touch both paper fastener tops at once. (If it is a bit small, wrap it in several layers of foil.) If you are using a marble, wrap it carefully in foil so it is completely covered and drop that in instead.

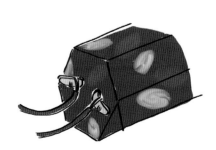

4 Cut off all the small flaps around the edge of the tube and then tape down the cardboard end of the tube (with the brads) with some sticky tape. The round heads of the brads will now be inside the tube and the pointed ends outside. Make sure that the pointed ends don't touch. Attach wires to the pointed ends.

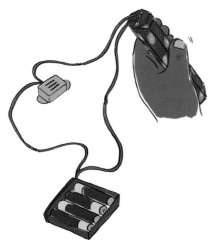

5 Attach the wires from the brads into the buzzer circuit and test the tilt switch. When you tilt the tube, the ball bearing/marble should roll down the tube and touch both brads at the same time. This will complete the circuit and the buzzer will go off.

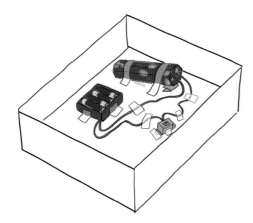

6 Tape the tube to the inside of the cookie tin. Raise the brad end slightly on some cardboard so the marble doesn't roll too soon. Tape the rest of the circuit into the tin.

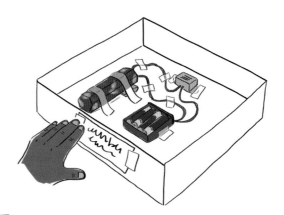

7 To make sure your victim lifts up the tin and tilts it, write a label to put on the side of the tin opposite where the brads are. How about: WARNING: READ CAREFULLY BEFORE OPENING! Your victim will pick up the tin, tilt it up to read it, and the buzzer should buzz! Finally, put on the cookie tin lid and invite your victim to eat a cookie from the tin.

wobbly clown and back-flipping clown

The first clown wibbles and wobbles but will never lie down. The second one does back flips all the way down a slope.

WOBBLY CLOWN

You will need

Table tennis ball

Sharp pointy scissors

Cardstock

Newspaper

Sticky tape

Marker pens

Modeling clay

A big marble

1 First cut the table tennis ball in half around the join line of the ball. You may need to ask an adult to help you cut it.

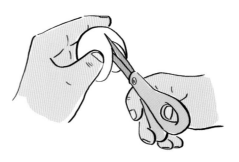

2 Cut a rectangle of cardstock that is 5 x 3 in. (12 x 8 cm).

3 Tightly roll up a piece of newspaper so that it is the same diameter as the table tennis ball and tuck the roll inside one of the ball halves (this is to make the next stage easier).

4 Cut a piece of sticky tape ready to use. Wrap the rectangle of cardstock around the newspaper and ball half and tape the cardstock together to make a tube.

5 Now tape around the join between the cardstock tube and the ball.

6 With the newspaper roll still inside to press against while you draw, draw a silly clown's face on the cardstock. Then take out the newspaper and try to stand him up. You'll find it is impossible!

7 Now roll some modeling clay into a ball that's a bit smaller than the half table tennis ball and drop it through the tube. Press it down so it sticks inside the bottom of the ball—you could use a pencil to push it down. Try standing your clown up now. You'll find he stands up easily but when you push him over he just pops up again—he won't stay lying down!

THE CLOWN THAT WON'T LIE DOWN

BACK-FLIPPING CLOWN

1 Take the modeling clay out of your wobbly clown and drop in the marble instead.

2 Tape the other half of the table tennis ball to the top of the cardstock tube.

3 Stand the clown at the top of a slight slope and give it a flick. Watch the clown do back flips all the way down the slope.

INSIDE THE SCIENCE
Gravity always pulls objects down toward the center of the Earth. In the clown with the modeling clay inside, almost all the weight is at the bottom—gravity pulls the bottom down and the clown stands upright. Because of its curved bottom, when you knock it over, with gravity still pulling the weight down, the clown's head flips up again. When you have the marble instead of the modeling clay inside, as soon as the clown starts moving the marble inside rolls from one end to the other, pulling first one end down and then the other, so he flips!

what's that wailing?

It's fun to do this experiment with friends. Find out who can get their coin spinning the fastest and loudest!

You will need

Large balloons—
light colored, almost
transparent ones
are best

Small coin

Balloon pump

Small metal hex (hexagonal)
nut

1 First, put the coin inside a deflated balloon.

2 Now inflate the balloon, as big as it can safely go, and tie it off with a knot.

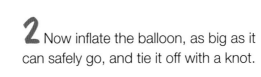

LET'S INVESTIGATE
Do small coins or large ones
spin for longer?
What happens with bigger or smaller
hex nuts or balloons—do you hear
different notes?
What happens if you put in more than
one coin or hex nut?

TRY THIS
Take another balloon and put the hex nut inside this one. Again, blow it up, nice and big, and tie it off. Spin this one in the same way—listen and feel the vibrations.

3 Hold the balloon upside down, with the knot under your palm. If the balloon slips, lick your fingers—they will stick. Now move the balloon around in a circle as if you were stirring a cake mix but much faster. You want to get the coin spinning around the edge of the balloon in a big circle. It takes a bit of practice.

4 Once the coin is spinning, hold the balloon still and watch the coin keeping spinning… and spinning… and spinning… How long does it keep going? What can you hear?

INSIDE THE SCIENCE

The coin or nut keeps spinning in a circle because of centripetal force, which means center-seeking force. The famous scientist, Sir Isaac Newton, explained it in his "first law of motion:" That a moving object keeps going in a straight line at the same speed unless another force acts on it. Our coin or hex nut is not going in a straight line, it's going in a circle. Something must be making that happen and we call it centripetal force.

The coin looks like a planet orbiting the sun and that's because planets are held in position by centripetal force, otherwise they would fly off into space—the coin would do the same if the balloon popped. Gravity holds planets in place; for the coin it is to do with the way it bounces on the sides of the balloon. The coin or nut slows down and falls eventually because of gravity, but it keeps going for a long time because the inside of the balloon is so smooth there isn't much friction to slow it down. The hex nut makes the weird sound because it vibrates against the balloon and vibrations cause sound waves.

how not to pop a balloon

Popping a balloon is easy—just push a pin into it. But what happens if you push it down onto lots of pins? If you don't like popping balloons, get some help while you cover your ears!

You will need

Safety goggles

Balloons

Balloon pump

Thumb tacks (drawing pins)

1 Inflate two balloons. Put on your safety goggles. Put one thumb tack (drawing pin) point up on a hard surface. Push balloon number 1 down onto the thumb tack. Get ready for the pop!

LET'S INVESTIGATE
The balloon pops with one thumb tack but doesn't pop with lots. How many thumb tacks do you need to have before it doesn't pop? To make it a fair test you need the same push on the balloon each time. Try putting the same heavy book on the balloon to push it onto the thumb tacks.

2 Now take a handful of thumb tacks— they must all be identical. Turn them all point up on the surface and gather them together into a small group.

3 Take balloon number 2 and push it down onto the thumb tacks. Push harder. How hard do you need to push before the balloon pops?

INSIDE THE SCIENCE

If you push a balloon down onto one thumb tack, all the force is on one tiny point, which easily makes a hole in the stretched rubber. Push the balloon onto lots of thumb tacks and the force is shared between lots of points, so the force with which each one pushes into the balloon is much less and is spread over a wider area: there isn't enough force to pop the balloon. Think about if you wanted to hammer a post into the ground. A flat wide end would be very difficult to hammer in, but a pointed end would go in easily because all the force is on a tiny spot.

skewer a balloon

Prick a balloon with a pin and it pops, so how is it possible that you can push a skewer right through a balloon without it bursting? Find out here, but take care with the sharp skewer.

You will need

Small balloons—the skewer should be longer than the balloons

Balloon pump

Long bamboo skewer

Sandpaper

Dish soap (washing-up liquid) or cooking oil

Safety goggles

1 Inflate a balloon until it is quite big and then let about a third of the air out before you tie it off.

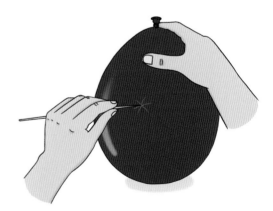

2 Use the sandpaper to smooth off and sharpen the point of the skewer. Rub a little dish soap (washing-up liquid) or cooking oil over the tip of the skewer to lubricate it (make it slippery).

LET'S INVESTIGATE
Use a marker pen to draw dots about ½ in. (1 cm) diameter all over an uninflated balloon. Make sure you make some around the neck and one at the very bottom. Inflate the balloon and look at what happens to the dots. Now can you see why you can skewer a balloon?

3 Put on your safety goggles. Slowly push the skewer into the side of the balloon—does it pop?

INSIDE THE SCIENCE

Balloons are made of latex and the molecules in latex are in long strands that stretch when you inflate the balloon. Look at the pattern of dots you made in "Let's Investigate" and you can see they have stretched a lot at the sides of the balloon but only a little at the top and by the neck. The ones at the sides are under lots of tension and they rip apart if you pierce them. The ones at the ends still have plenty of stretch in them and will simply stretch around the skewer when you pierce the balloon.

4 Inflate another balloon. Still wearing your safety goggles, slowly but firmly push the skewer into the balloon just beside the tied-off neck, twisting it a little from side to side as you push. It should push through. Keep pushing the skewer right through the balloon to the very bottom and push it out of the other side. The balloon will stay inflated. You can even pull the skewer out and the balloon will only deflate slowly.

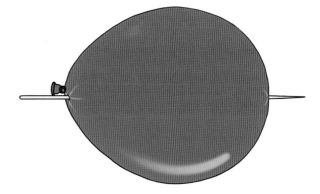

balloon rocket

This balloon rocket is easy to make, but it really does go! Try making one in your backyard with a good long piece of kite string or fishing line, or you can do it indoors, but get an adult's permission first! This project is much easier with a friend to help you.

You will need

About 16 ft (4.5 m) of kite string or fishing line—the smoother the string, the faster your rocket will go

Drinking straw

Balloon—the long torpedo-shaped ones are best

Balloon pump

Sticky tape

1 Choose two objects to tie the string to—for example, garden chairs, trees, or fences. They should be about 10–15 ft (3–5 m) apart, but they don't have to be at exactly the same height—your rocket can fly uphill or downhill. Tie one end of the string to one of the objects.

TRY THIS
If you have enough space, try having a balloon rocket race with another line of string and a second balloon.

2 Thread the other end of the string through the drinking straw.

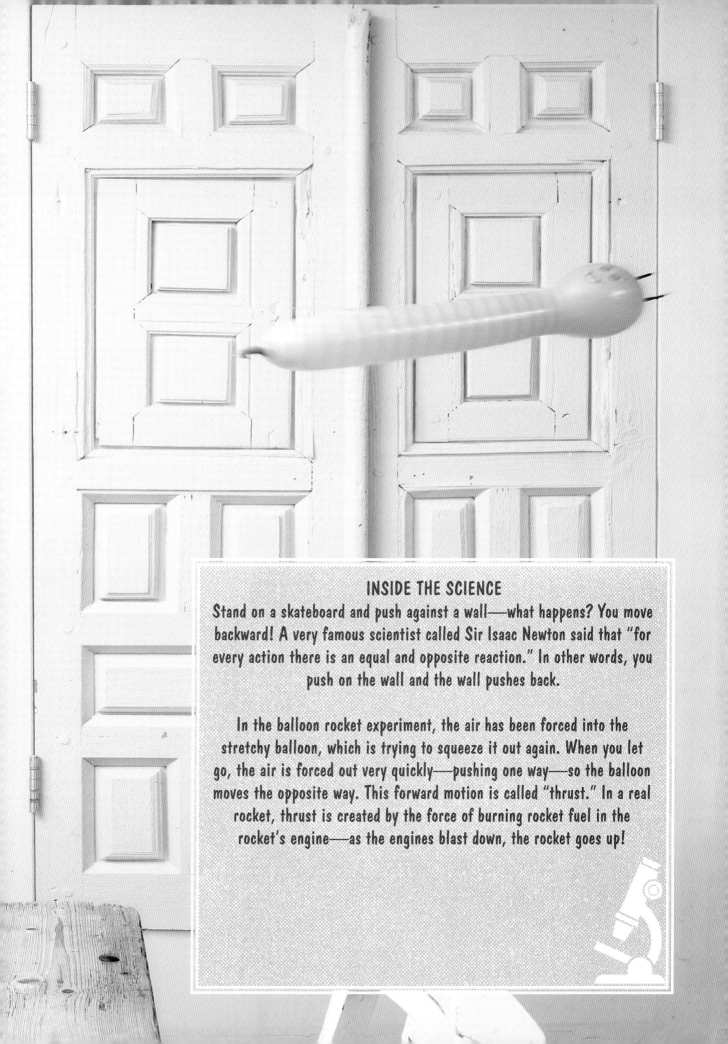

INSIDE THE SCIENCE

Stand on a skateboard and push against a wall—what happens? You move backward! A very famous scientist called Sir Isaac Newton said that "for every action there is an equal and opposite reaction." In other words, you push on the wall and the wall pushes back.

In the balloon rocket experiment, the air has been forced into the stretchy balloon, which is trying to squeeze it out again. When you let go, the air is forced out very quickly—pushing one way—so the balloon moves the opposite way. This forward motion is called "thrust." In a real rocket, thrust is created by the force of burning rocket fuel in the rocket's engine—as the engines blast down, the rocket goes up!

3 Now get your friend to help you pull the string as tight as possible while you tie it to the other object.

4 Inflate the balloon—using a balloon pump if you have one—but don't knot it. Twist the end and hold it closed while your friend tapes the straw to the balloon in two different places. The balloon opening will be the back of the rocket so make sure the front is facing along the string.

5 To launch your rocket; simply let the end of the balloon go and see it shoot along the string!

LET'S INVESTIGATE
You can launch your rocket over and over again and use a stopwatch to time the results. Try it with different shaped balloons—which shape goes fastest or furthest? Does the angle of the string make a difference? Does the length of the straw make a difference? Try it using a different type of twine or string.

electric balloon

Static electricity can make your hair stand on end when you take off a sweater. It can make sparks fly when you run along a carpeted corridor and then kiss someone. It sticks clothes together in a tumble drier, and it can also make balloons have strange powers. Find out about some of them.

You will need

Balloons

Balloon pump

Twine, string, or yarn

Empty aluminum soda can

1 Inflate two balloons and then rub each one on your hair for a little while. As you lift them away your hair will follow the balloon and stand on end. If it doesn't, rub a bit more.

2 Tie a string to each balloon. Hold one in each hand and bring them together. Can you make them touch?

3 Put a can on its side. Now hold a balloon near to, but not touching, the side of the can. Will the can follow the balloon when you move it slowly backward?

LET'S INVESTIGATE
Inflate more balloons and try rubbing each one on different surfaces—carpet, a woolen sweater, a cotton sweatshirt, and a polyester shirt—before trying the trick again. Which surface makes the can or water move most? If you put a few drops of water in the can to increase its weight will it still move? How much can you add before it is too heavy to move?

4 Rub the balloon on your hair again to build up some more static charge. Turn on a faucet (tap) until there is a small but steady trickle of cold water (not drops). Slowly move the balloon toward the water, but don't touch it. Did you see the water bend? If it didn't, try rubbing the balloon some more and have an even smaller stream of water.

INSIDE THE SCIENCE

This experiment involves electricity! An object can be negatively charged, positively charged, or neutral (no charge). Objects with the same charge repel each other, which means push each other away (a bit like magnets do). Objects with different charges attract. If one object is charged and the other isn't, they also attract.

When you rub the balloon on your hair, negatively charged electrons jump from your hair to the balloon so the balloon is negatively charged— this is static electricity. Since the other balloon is also negatively charged, the two balloons will push away from each other. When an object has no charge, it means that positive and negative charges are cancelling each other out, so taking away negatively charged electrons from your hair

leaves behind a positive charge. Since negative attracts positive, your hair is attracted to the balloon and stands on end. The same happens with the can and the water. Both of them are neutral so are attracted to the negatively charged balloon: The water bends and the can rolls.

black and white balloons

Have you ever been told that wearing white clothes will keep you cooler on a hot day, or that if the ice caps melt the world will get warmer because ice reflects more heat than water? This dramatic balloon experiment, which you need to do on a sunny day with a helper, will make you believe it.

You will need

Black balloon, white balloon, balloons in other colors (all the balloons should be the same shape and size)

Balloon pump

Twine or string

Two pairs of safety goggles

Magnifying glass

Second timer

1 Choose a sunny day. Inflate the balloons until they are all a similar size and tie them off. Tie strings to them and then take them outside and tie them to a chair or railings so they don't blow away.

2 Both you and your helper should put on safety goggles. Take the white balloon. Hold the magnifying glass and focus the sun's rays onto the side of the white balloon. You need to move it backward and forward toward the balloon until you get a small dot of really intense light. Hold it there for 10 seconds (count out loud). Does anything happen to the balloon?

3 Now take the black balloon. Focus the sun onto it and begin timing. How far can you count before the balloon bursts? Keep going with the other balloons.

WHICH COLOR BURSTS FIRST?

LET'S INVESTIGATE
Keep a record of how long it takes before the balloons burst. Which colors burst quickly? Which hold out for longer? Why?

INSIDE THE SCIENCE

We see when light bounces (reflects) off an object into our eyes. White light is a mixture of all the colors of the rainbow. When we see a white object, we are seeing all the colors mixed together reflecting off the object. When we see a colored object, we are seeing that color reflected while all the other colors are absorbed by it (go into it). When something is black, it means all the colors are absorbed and nothing is reflected. (A hole in a closed box looks black because all the light goes into the box and nothing comes out.)

When you focus the sunlight onto the white balloon, it is mostly reflected and the balloon doesn't heat up, the rubber doesn't melt, and the balloon doesn't burst. When you focus sunlight on the black balloon, most of the light is absorbed. The energy in the light causes the balloon to heat up and the rubber melts— bang! The other colored balloons will absorb some of the sunlight, so they may take a little longer to burst than the black one.

hovering helium

Air-filled balloons are great for playing games with because when you hit them up they come back down again. With helium balloons things are different; let one go outside, and it will fly into the air and disappear.

You will need

Store-bought helium balloon with a string or ribbon

Lots of paper clips

Sticky tack

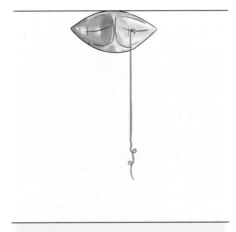

1 Once you are in the house, take any weights off the string of the balloon and let it go. Watch it sail up until it hits the ceiling.

STAY SAFE
Don't take your foil balloon outside in case it floats away. Escaped foil balloons can be dangerous if they hit power lines and all balloons can harm wildlife when they eventually come back to earth.

2 Catch the string and slide on paper clips until the balloon sinks down and the string touches the floor.

INSIDE THE SCIENCE

Helium gas is lighter than air so a balloon filled with helium gas weighs less than the air that would have filled the space taken up by the balloon. This means that the helium will float, just like a piece of wood will float on water. The difference is that the water has a surface—the water pushes the wood up until it floats on the surface. Air has no surface so the helium balloon will keep rising until the air thins out higher in the atmosphere and the weight of the helium equals the weight of the air it has displaced. The balloons deflate and sink after a while because there are tiny spaces between the molecules of the balloon through which the helium molecules can escape.

3 Now take off one paper clip—does the balloon rise to the ceiling again or can you get it to hover so the balloon doesn't touch the ceiling and the string doesn't touch the floor? Use little balls of sticky tack attached to a paper clip to get it exactly right, hanging in space.

LET'S INVESTIGATE

Let the balloon hang in space. How long will it float before it sinks to the floor? Get two helium balloons—an ordinary latex balloon and a shiny foil balloon. Get them both to hang in space. Which do you think will drop to the ground first? If you can get quite a lot of helium balloons, find out how many are needed to lift a favorite toy off the ground for a balloon ride.

weighing air

Does air really weigh something? Lift your hand up—you can't feel any air pressing down on it. If you did the same in water, you would feel the weight of water. Here is a way of proving that air does weigh something.

You will need

String or yarn

Length of dowel (round wood) or bamboo skewer about 12 in. (30 cm) long

Two balloons

Balloon pump

Pin

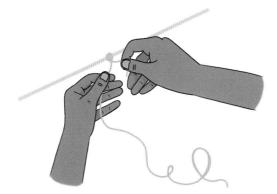

1 Cut a piece of string about 12 in. (30 cm) long. Wrap one end tightly around the center of the dowel three or four times and tie a tight knot.

2 Tie the other end to the handle of a high kitchen cabinet so the dowel hangs freely below it. Push the string along the dowel (it should still be tight and difficult to move) until the dowel is balanced and horizontal.

CAN YOU FEEL THE PRESSURE?

3 Inflate the two balloons with a balloon pump until they are the same size and tie them off. Don't blow them up or you will be weighing the gas you breathe out, which isn't the same as air! Tie short lengths of string to each of them and then tie them tightly to the two ends of the dowel. Move the balloons along the dowel until they are balanced and the dowel is horizontal again. (Moving a balloon toward the center will make it appear to weigh less.)

LET'S INVESTIGATE
Try the experiment with two identical ziplock bags—one flat and one blown up with air. They will weigh the same. The balloon experiment works because a lot of air is forced into the stretchy balloon under high pressure. This air is denser (has more molecules in it) than in the surrounding air.

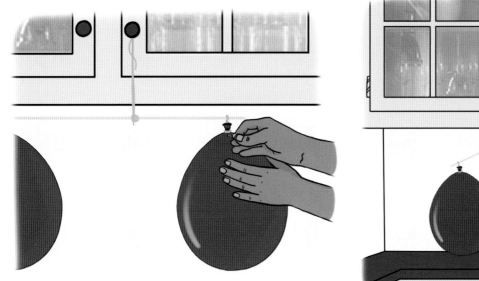

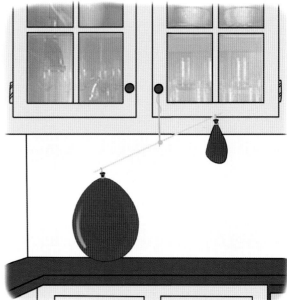

4 Use the pin to carefully pierce one balloon near the tied knot (see page 75). You don't want the balloon to burst suddenly but to let the air out slowly. If it is being very slow make a few more holes.

5 Watch as the balloon deflates. The burst balloon will rise up and the inflated balloon will drop, showing it is now heavier: Air has weight!

INSIDE THE SCIENCE

Air is made up of different invisible gases. Dry air is nearly 80 percent nitrogen and 20 percent oxygen, with tiny amounts of argon and carbon dioxide. Most air also contains water vapor—if the day is described as humid, it means there is a lot of water in the air. All this gas presses down on you. That pressure is called air pressure.

Imagine a square with sides of 1 in. (2.5 cm). A column of air on top of that square inch which reaches from sea level to the top of the Earth's atmosphere would have a weight of about 14.7 lb (6.67 kg). (If you go up a mountain, there is less air above you so the air pressure is less.) That weight is pressing down on you all the time from all directions but since you have never known any different you don't feel it. This experiment proves it weighs something!

freshwater wizardry

Imagine being adrift on the ocean or stranded on a desert island with no fresh water. Here's a bit of science that could help you survive, although you might not have quite the same equipment in your boat or on your island! This is a project to do outside on a hot, sunny day.

You will need

Large glass or china bowl— a glass one will make it easier to see what is going on

Small glass tumbler—not as tall as the bowl

A pitcher (jug)

Water

Tablespoon

Salt

Spoon for stirring

Plastic wrap (clingfilm)

1 Ask permission to use the bowl first and be very careful not to drop it. A glass or china bowl is better than plastic because the plastic wrap will cling to it. Find a hot sunny place to put the bowl, where it won't be in the way or get knocked over. Place the glass in the middle of the bowl.

2 Fill the pitcher (jug) with water and add several tablespoons of salt. Stir the water well to dissolve the salt.

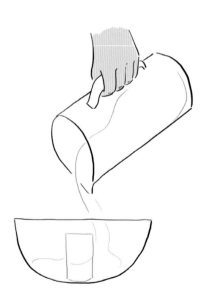

3 Pour the water into the bowl around the glass.

4 Cover the bowl with plastic wrap (clingfilm), making sure that it is sealed so that no air can get in or out.

5 Gently press down in the center of the plastic wrap above the glass to make the plastic dip down a little there. Be careful not to make a hole.

6 Leave the bowl all day or for several days. Fresh, unsalty water will slowly collect in the glass.

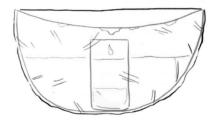

LEARN A SURVIVAL TECHNIQUE

making rainbows

Think about all the many different places you have seen rainbows: up in the sky when the sun is shining after a storm; in a puddle covered with a film of oil; in bubbles; on CDs left in the sun; on the walls of your house when the sun is shining through a hanging crystal or a crystal vase. Can you think of any other places you have seen them? This project shows you two ways to make rainbows of your own.

You will need

Garden hose

Sunny day

or

Flashlight (torch)

Black paper

Pencil

Scissors

Sticky tape

Plastic food box

Water

Small mirror—a purse mirror is ideal

White card

SUNNY DAY METHOD

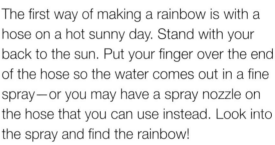

The first way of making a rainbow is with a hose on a hot sunny day. Stand with your back to the sun. Put your finger over the end of the hose so the water comes out in a fine spray—or you may have a spray nozzle on the hose that you can use instead. Look into the spray and find the rainbow!

INDOOR METHOD

1 If it is not hot and sunny, make a rainbow in a dark room or even inside a dark cupboard! Put the flashlight (torch) face down on a piece of black paper and use a pencil to draw around the face of the flashlight.

2 Cut out the circle. Fold the circle in half and cut out a tiny hole in the middle. Tape the circle over the face of the flashlight.

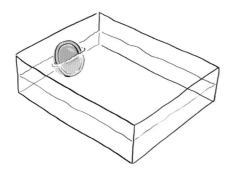

3 Half fill the box with water and stand the mirror in the box so that it is leaning against one end at an angle, half in the water.

4 Switch out all the lights. Shine the flashlight through the water onto the part of the mirror that is underwater.

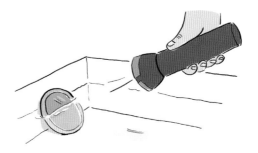

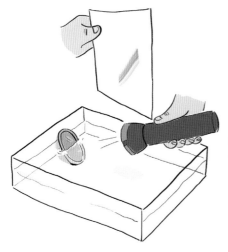

5 Hold the white cardboard up to catch the light that is reflecting off the mirror—look for the rainbow!

"RED AND YELLOW AND PINK AND GREEN..."

ice cream science

On the whole, eating and science projects don't mix—you should never taste anything in a science laboratory—but in this project you can use the power of salt to freeze your own ice cream and then you can eat it! Even better, if you are doing this in the winter and there is snow on the ground, you can use snow from your backyard instead of the ice cubes!

You will need

For the ice cream mix:

½ cup (120 ml) milk

½ cup (120 ml) heavy (double) cream

¼ cup (50 g) sugar

¼ teaspoon vanilla extract

Measuring cup and spoon

Pitcher (jug)

Spoon for stirring

To freeze the ice cream:

1-quart (2-pint) ziplock freezer bag, about 7 x 8 in. (18 x 20 cm)

A pair of warm gloves

2–3 cups of ice cubes

Clean dish towel

Rolling pin

1-gallon (8-pint) ziplock freezer bag, about 10 x 11 in. (25 x 27.5 cm)

Thermometer (optional)

½–¾ cup (120–180 g) salt

1 Put the milk, cream, sugar, and vanilla extract into the jug (pitcher) and give everything a good stir.

2 Pour this ice cream mixture into the smaller ziplock bag, squeeze out the air, and zip it closed.

3 Put on your gloves and ask an adult to help you take ice cubes from the freezer. (Don't touch them with bare hands or they could stick to your skin and hurt it.) Pile the ice cubes onto a clean dish towel. Wrap them up and gently bash them with a rolling pin to crush them.

4 Put about 2 cups of crushed ice (or snow) into the large ziplock bag. If you have a thermometer, measure the temperature of the ice.

5 Add the salt to the ice and, with your gloves still on, mush the outside of the bag a bit to mix the salt and ice.

INSIDE THE SCIENCE

Ice needs energy (heat) to change from a solid to a liquid. If you put plain ice around the ice cream mix, the ice would take warmth from the mix and cool it—but not enough to freeze it. Salt lowers the freezing point of ice, so if you add salt to ice it will need even more energy (heat) to melt it. It takes all this energy from the ice cream, making it cold enough to freeze into ice cream. When you measure the temperature of the ice the second time, it will be much lower than the first time!

6 Still with your gloves on, put the bag with ice cream mix in it inside the bag with the ice. Make sure the smaller bag is surrounded by ice and salt. Squeeze out the air and zip seal the big bag. Still wearing gloves, gently squeeze and massage the ice around the inner bag. Keep doing this for about 10–15 minutes.

7 Check it! The ice cream mix in the inner bag will have frozen into ice cream, even though you haven't put it in the freezer! Still wearing gloves, take the ice cream bag out of the bigger bag. Measure the temperature of the ice again and then eat your ice cream!

MASH UP SOME ICE CREAM

water rocket

5 – 4 – 3 – 2 – 1 blast off! You will not believe how high you can make a plastic bottle fly or the feeling of suspense as you wait for it to launch. To make a water rocket you will have to buy a Rokit kit (or ask for one for a birthday present) but it is well worth it and it can be used over and over again.

You will need

A Rokit water rocket kit (available from www.rokit.com)

Bucket of water and a pitcher (jug)

Large plastic fizzy drink bottle (1 or 2-quart/liter is ideal)— check that the Rokit collar fits the bottle

Bicycle pump (a floor pump is best)

Large, safe, open area for launching—check that there are no overhead power lines

Stopwatch (optional)

1 Always ask an adult to help you. Following the instructions in the Rokit kit, put together the parts of the collar and attach the fins to it. Pour water into the bottle until it is about a quarter full and screw on the collar. Attach the screw end of the yellow pressure tube to a bicycle pump and push the brass plug, on the other end, into the hole in the black rubber nozzle in the collar.

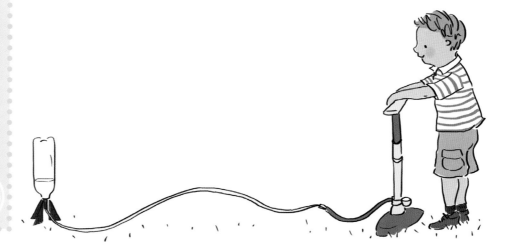

2 Turn the rocket over so it is standing on its fins and position on some firm, flat ground. Step back as far as you can—the hose is quite long—and begin pumping. You will see the air bubbling up through the water but it is hard to guess when the rocket will take off! If you are too close, you will get showered with water.

INSIDE THE SCIENCE

When you pump air into the bottle the pressure inside rises. It keeps rising until it is strong enough to force the end of the hose out through the rubber nozzle. The water is also forced out of the hole in the nozzle. The force of the water pushing downward produces thrust in the opposite direction (see page 77) so the rocket shoots up against the force of gravity. After a few seconds the thrust gets weaker until gravity is as strong as the thrust so the rocket reaches its highest point. Then gravity pulls the rocket back down to earth. A parachute would slow the rocket down by increasing air resistance. A nose cone could make the rocket more streamlined so it might go higher. The fins add stability so it flies straighter.

3 Now you can begin some real science. It is quite difficult to measure how high the rocket goes but you can time how long it stays in the air. You and your friends could hold a competition. You could each make a custom-built rocket and then see which one stays up for longest. Try adding a nose cone or bigger fins. Can you design a parachute that will let it drop back to earth more slowly? Is it better to have more water or less water in the bottle?

WE HAVE LIFT OFF!

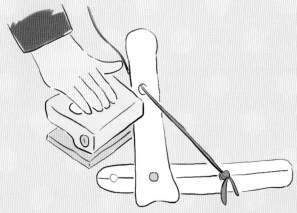

CHAPTER THREE
amazing bodies

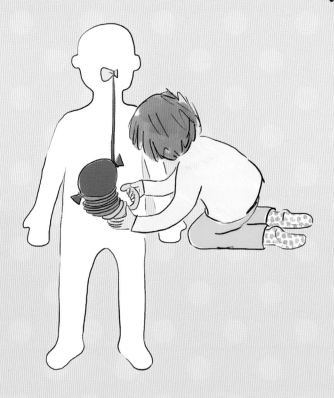

pinhole camera

Discover how your pupils work by making a pinhole camera—it's easier than it sounds! You'll need to look out for one of the round snack tubes that have a metal base and a plastic lid.

You will need

Long potato chip tube (or other tube with metal at one end and a plastic lid)

Ruler

Pencil

Sharp scissors

Thumb tack (drawing pin)

Hammer

Greaseproof paper

Sticky parcel tape

Aluminum foil

Magnifying glass

1 First take the snack tube and measure 2 in. (5 cm) from the metal end in several places around the tube. Join up the marks to make a line. Use a sharp pair of scissors and cut around the line (or ask an adult to use a craft knife).

2 Push the thumb tack (drawing pin) through the center of the metal end to make a tiny hole. Tap it gently with a hammer, if you need to. If the plastic lid is transparent (you can see through it), draw around it on the greaseproof paper and cut out the circle. Place the paper circle inside the lid and then put the lid on the short section you have just cut. Miss out this stage if the lid is translucent (cloudy) plastic.

3 Use the sticky tape to join the two parts of the tube together again with the lid between them. The lid makes a screen inside.

4 Wrap a piece of foil all around the tube and tape it together to keep all the light out of the tube.

5 Now hold the open end of the tube up to your eye and point the hole toward a bright window (never directly toward the sun) or lamp. Hold it tight against your face so no light gets inside. You should see a tiny image of the lamp or the scene from the window on the screen inside the tube—but it will be upside down! This is exactly what happens in your eye. The light from outside passes through the pupil and makes an upside down image on the retina at the back of your eye.

6 Now put a magnifying glass in front of the hole. You may have to move it forward and back a little, but at some point you should a get a much brighter, clearer image of the upside-down lamp or window on the screen. This is called focusing. There is a lens inside your eye just like this. It doesn't move around, but muscles pull it so it gets wider or thinner and that has the same effect as moving it. The lens is there to make sure that the image is focused on your retina. If it's not, everything you see will be blurry and you will need glasses—which are extra lenses—to help get the image to the correct place.

INSIDE THE SCIENCE
The image is upside down and you don't see the world upside down, so what happens? Your brain makes sure you see the right way up! The light rays hit special cells in your retina and these send tiny electrical signals along the optic nerve to your brain. The nerve is like the cable running to your television. The picture isn't in the cable; it's just a coded signal—it needs the electronics inside the television to turn the code into a picture. In the same way, your eye needs the supercomputer that is your brain to make you see.

smell test

Try this smell test to find out how good your sense of smell is—you'll need a friend to help you as you have to smell each item blindfolded!

You will need

Lots of different smelly items – here are some ideas:

—orange peel

—lemon peel

—pine needles

—coffee beans/powder

—tea leaves

—garlic

—onion

—vinegar

—mint leaves or other herbs

—rose petals

—pencil shavings

—perfume

—vanilla extract

—potato chips (crisps)

—sawdust Blindfold

About 10 foil cake cases or mini plastic pots

Cotton balls

Sticky labels

Pen

Notebook, pencil, and ruler

1 Put a small sample of each of the different smelly materials into the cupcake cases. Label them so you don't forget what they contain. For liquids such as perfume, vinegar, and vanilla extract, put a few drops onto a small piece of cotton ball and put the cotton ball into a cake case. For mint, or other herbs, and pine needles crush the leaves a little before you put them in the pot to release the smell. Peel and crush a garlic clove. Cut off a small slice of onion.

2 To make the test into a proper scientific experiment, make a list of all the different smells in your notebook and draw columns beside the list, with one column for each member of your family or for each of your friends.

3 When everything is ready, blindfold someone, and let them smell each of the pots in turn. Tick the ones they can identify. Ask someone to blindfold you too so you can try, although it won't really be fair because you know what you put in the pots! Which smells were easiest to identify? Who had the best sense of smell?

FASCINATING FACTS
Every taste you recognize is a combination of these sweet, sour, salty, bitter, and savory, but flavor also depends on all those thousands of different smells you can identify, which is why food doesn't taste right when you have a blocked-up nose. We have 5–6 million smell-detecting cells but dogs have about 220 million, which is why dogs follow their noses!

HEALTH TIPS

We all love the taste of sweet foods like soda (fizzy drinks), candy (sweets), and cookies, but our sense of taste tricks us into eating too much of something that is bad for us. Too much sugar can lead to tooth decay and make you put on weight. If you're aged 7–10 you shouldn't have more than six teaspoons of sugar in your food a day, but there's about nine teaspoons of sugar in just one can of soda! Sugar can be hidden in lots of foods—take a look at the ingredients of your cereal, pasta sauce, or yogurt: How much sugar do they contain?

Don't pick your nose—this can lead to nose bleeds (and it looks disgusting!).

Use-by dates on fresh food help keep us safe from food that has gone bad but always sniff food and if something doesn't smell right, don't eat it.

air pressure and ears

If you have been on a plane, you will have felt your ears hurting or popping on take-off and landing. Low-pressure air in the airplane makes this happen. Try this experiment to see how.

You will need

Sturdy plastic drinks bottle with lid (not one of the really weak ones)

Large bowl

Kettle

1 Stand the bottle in the bowl. Boil a kettle and ask an adult to pour about 1 in. (2.5 cm) of boiling water into the bottle. Wait for about 15 seconds and then put the lid on the bottle.

2 Add some cold water to the bowl and watch what happens. The bottle should cave in and crumple! This is because steam from the boiling water pushed out the air. When the steam cooled and turned back to water, there wasn't as much air in the bottle so the air pressure was lower. The higher air pressure outside the bottle pushed in the plastic.

INSIDE THE SCIENCE

The middle ear is like the bottle. There is a narrow tube that runs from your middle ear to the back of the throat called the eustachian tube. It opens when you swallow, yawn, or chew. When you fly on a plane, the tube will open and let the lower pressure air from the plane into your ear. When you land, the air pressure in the plane returns to normal and pushes on your eardrum like it did the plastic bottle. To stop it hurting, yawn or chew gum. Alternatively, close your mouth, hold your nose, and gently breathe in through your nose to equalize the pressure inside your ears and out. (When you take off, the higher pressure inside your ear pushes from the inside out.)

taste test

How well do you know your fruits? Find out how much taste is linked to smell with this simple test.

You will need

Crisp apple

Crisp pear

Peeler

Cutting board

Knife

1 Peel the apple and the pear. Place them on a chopping board and chop them into pieces that are roughly the same size and shape. Separate the pear pieces and apple pieces on the board. Remember which is which.

2 Get some friends or members of your family to hold their noses, so they can't smell, and give them a cube of apple or pear to eat. Can they identify which it is? Get them to try it on you. Identifying taste isn't easy without smell!

EYED CLOSED. NO PEEKING!

how good is your sense of touch?

**A touch can be painful like a sting or soft like the feel of fur.
Nerves in your skin feel and send the information to your brain.**

You will need

Paper clip

Blindfold

Friend or family member

The nerve endings in your skin send messages to your brain whenever they sense touch, heat, cold, or pain. When you stand, nerves in your feet feel the ground, when you sit your body feels the chair, when you pick something up you know how firmly to hold it and, if it's hot, you know to drop it. Nerve endings fire with pain when you bang your funny bone or cut your knee. Our nerves keep us safe. However, in some areas of your body there are many more nerve endings than in others. Can you guess which have the most? Think about what you do when you want to find out about the texture, temperature, weight, or shape of an object. Now think what a baby does. That will give you some clues about which parts have the most nerve endings.

1 Unbend the paper clip and then bend it into a U shape with the two points about ½ in. (1 cm) apart.

2 Put a blindfold on your friend. Gently press the two ends of the paper clip on the skin of their arm. Be sure the two ends touch at the same time. Ask them if they can feel two points or one. (If you think they might cheat and say two when they only feel one, do it a few times and sometimes press with just one point.) Now try it somewhere else—try the palm of their hand, fingertip, top lip, cheek, and leg. Find out which areas on their body can feel two points easily. Now swap and let them try it on you. If you are being properly scientific, record your findings in your notebook.

3 Experiment a bit further. Pull the ends of the paper clip apart a little and try again in one of the places where your friend could only feel one point. Keep widening the gap until they feel two points. Record what you have found out.

LET'S INVESTIGATE
Scientists have found out that you can feel two points on your fingertips when the points are only a tiny distance apart. Your upper lip is almost as good but on your leg the points need to be more than 1½ in. (4 cm) apart before you can feel them both.
Do you agree?

temperature test

One way our skin protects is by letting us know when things are very hot and will burn us or very cold, which can damage skin. But just how good are we at judging how hot something is? Do this activity to find out.

You will need

3 big bowls

Hot and cold water

Some ice cubes

1 Fill one bowl with hot water from the faucet (tap). Add a little cold and then dip your finger into it quickly. If it feels too hot, you know your nerve endings are doing their job well and warning you that you will burn your skin if you put your hand in it. Add more cold water a little at a time until it is still hot but your hand feels comfortable in it.

2 Fill another bowl with cold water and add some ice cubes. Dip your finger in this one. If it hurts it's too cold—again your nerves are doing their job well. Take out the ice cubes and add a bit of hot water so you can just bear to have your hand in it. Put the hot and cold bowls side by side on the kitchen surface.

NOT TOO HOT, NOT TOO COLD!

3 Fill the third bowl with some lukewarm water—a mixture of hot and cold from the faucet (tap).

4 Put one hand in the hot bowl and the other hand in the cold bowl and leave them there while you count to 60.

5 Now put both hands together in the lukewarm water. How does it feel? For the hand that has been in cold water it should feel warm, for the hand that has been in hot water it should feel cold! Our skins are good at protecting us from burning or freezing ourselves, but are not much good at being thermometers and measuring temperature. You know this from swimming—on a hot day a pool can feel freezing, but if you are cold, the same temperature pool feels lovely and warm.

INSIDE THE SCIENCE
There are different types of nerves doing different jobs in your skin. The nerves that detect cold don't work when the temperature drops below 41°F (5°C), which is why your hands and feet go numb when they are very cold. The nerves that detect heat don't work above 113°F (45°C) because then the nerves that detect pain take over to tell you that your skin is too hot and will burn.

draw your own skeleton

How well do you know your own body? Here is an activity for you to get to know it a bit better. You will need a friend to help you with this one and, by the end, you will have a full-sized picture of your skeleton. Remember that bones can't bend. Wherever parts of your body bend, there must be a joint between two bones.

You will need

Roll of wallpaper

Marker pens

Full-length mirror

Friend

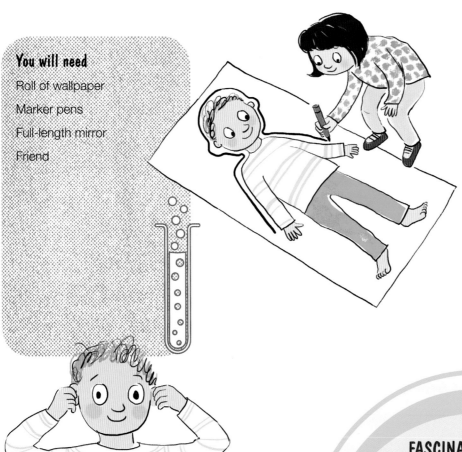

1 Cut one length of wallpaper as tall as you are and one as tall as your friend. One of you should lie down on the plain side of your paper while the other draws all the way around you. Then swap so you have outlines of both your bodies.

2 Feel your skull. Are your nose, ears, and eyes made of hard bone? Feel the bony ridges around your eyes. How big are the hollow eye sockets your eyes fit in? Open your mouth. Feel where your jawbone attaches to your skull. Draw your skull inside the head of your outline. Your skull protects your brain.

FASCINATING FACTS
The longer astronauts live in space without gravity, the weaker their bones become. This could be a problem for space travel to Mars!

3 Feel the back of your neck and find your spine (back bone). Now run your fingers as far up and down your spine as you can. What does it feel like? Can you count how many bones make up your spine? Where does it end? Draw it in. Your spine holds you up.

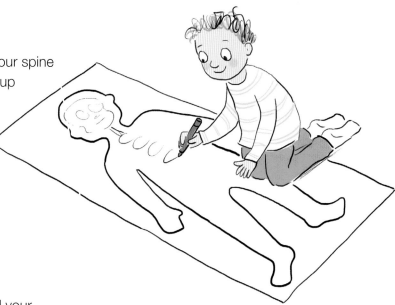

4 Feel either side of your spine and find your sticking-out shoulder blades. What shape do you think they are? Draw them in?

5 Feel around the front of your neck and your shoulders and look in the mirror. What bones can you see and feel? You need bones in your shoulders to join your arms on to. Draw them in.

6 Look in the mirror. Pull your shirt up and pull in your tummy as hard as you can. Can you see your ribs? Count them if you can. Your ribs protect your heart and lungs and help you breathe. Draw them.

7 Lie on your back and feel your hip bones. You need your hip bones to hold your insides up and to join your legs on to. Draw them in.

8 Now for your legs. How many bones can you feel in your leg above your knee? How many below it? Can you find your kneecaps. Draw in your leg bones.

9 Feet are very complicated. Take off your shoes and socks and have a feel. How many bones do you think are in your foot and how many are in each toe? (Hint: You might not be able to feel them all, but it's more than 20!) Draw your feet.

10 Now do your arms and hands in the same way, carefully checking the number of bones in your fingers and thumb.

11 Stand back and admire your drawing, then turn to the diagram on page 114 and see how well you have done. Why not cut out the outline and hang it up?

joint quiz

A joint is where two bones meet. If our skeleton was all one piece we wouldn't be able to move and bend. There are lots of different types of joints in our bodies, but this quiz is just about two important ones.

Ball and socket joint
Imagine a big, round candy on a stick (lollipop) inside half a table tennis ball that just fits around it. The stick can move in all directions as the candy (lollipop) turns in the ball.

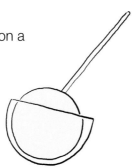

Hinge joint
Think about opening and closing the lid of a hinged box. That's all the lid can do—open and close. It can't move any other way.

Now try the quiz. Move your arms, legs, and fingers around and decide whether you have a ball and socket joint or a hinge joint in these five places.

1 In your shoulder
2 In the middle of your finger
3 In your elbow
4 Between your leg and your body (your hip joint)
5 In your knee

(answers at the bottom of the page)

FASCINATING FACTS
When people say they are double-jointed it means they have extra-long ligaments. Ligaments hold your joints together. If your ligaments are longer and more stretchy, you can bend your joints further.

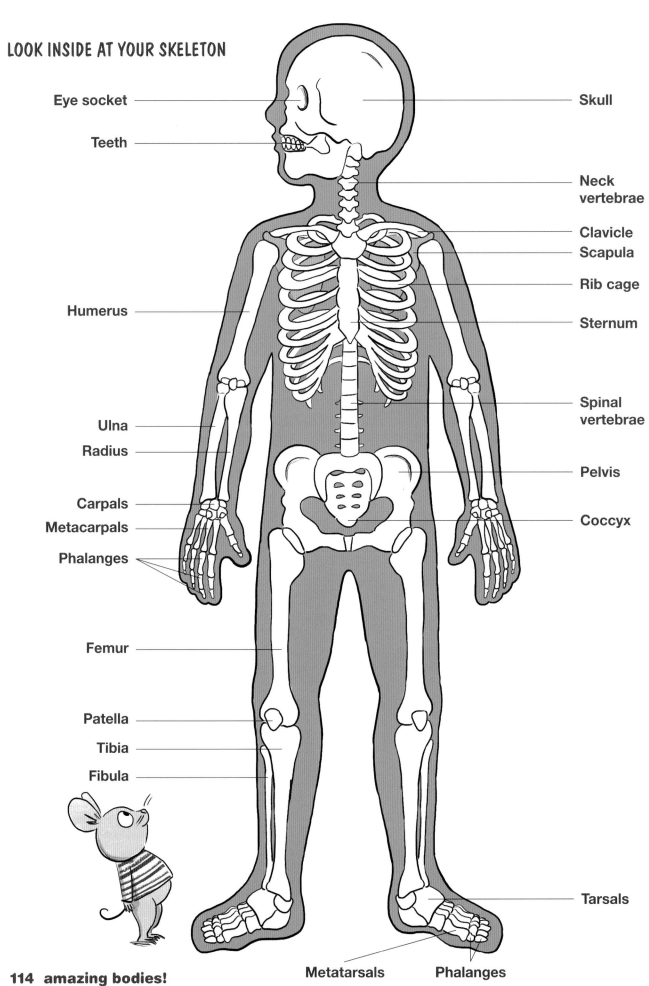

LOOK INSIDE AT YOUR SKELETON

Eye socket

Teeth

Humerus

Ulna

Radius

Carpals

Metacarpals

Phalanges

Femur

Patella

Tibia

Fibula

Skull

Neck vertebrae

Clavicle

Scapula

Rib cage

Sternum

Spinal vertebrae

Pelvis

Coccyx

Tarsals

Metatarsals

Phalanges

114 amazing bodies!

flexible spine

Your spine holds you up so it needs to be strong, but it also needs to be flexible so you can bend. Try making this easy model of a spine.

As well as holding you up, your spine has another really important job. It's there to protect your spinal cord—a bundle of nerves that run from the brain. It is the main communication cable to the brain. All your other nerves branch off the spinal cord.

It's easy to make a model of a spine to show how it works. In the model the washing line is like the spinal cord and each egg cup is like one vertebra. See how it can only bend a little between each "vertebra," but each little bend adds to a complete bend. Your spine has 26 not 12 vertebrae, but some of the ones at the base of the spine are fused together to make one bone that does not bend. You even have a little tail of fused vertebra at the base of your spine called the coccyx.

You will need

Large egg carton

Sharp pointy scissors

Wooden skewer (or a knitting needle)

Piece of plastic-coated washing line

1 Cut up the egg carton so you have 12 separate cups.

2 Carefully push the skewer right through each egg box cup so it goes in one side of the cup and out of the other, making two holes. Wiggle it around to make the holes bigger or use the point of your scissors.

3 Thread the washing line through each hole. When you have finished, line up the egg carton cups so they are all bottom up.

4 Push the cups close together. Wind some sticky tape around the washing line where it goes into the first cup and where it comes out of the last one to stop the cups moving around and slipping on the washing line. Now bend your model around to see how it curves over and back and to the side.

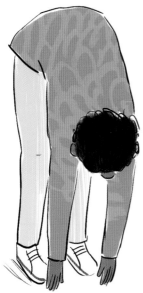

5 Now see how flexible your own spine is. Bend forward—can you touch your toes without bending your knees? Bend your model to match the different poses.

6 Bend backward as if you are limbo dancing or, starting from lying on the ground, see if you can arch up into a crab position.

7 Stand with your legs a little apart, stretch up tall with your left arm, then slide your right arm down your right leg as you bend to the side. How far can you bend? Try on both sides.

8 Sit cross-legged. Put your right hand on your left knee and your left hand on the floor behind you—twist round as far as you can. Now do it on the other side. How far can you twist?

robot hand

This robot hand model will help you to see how bones and muscles work together—and you could even play tricks on your friends with it later! The model doesn't include the carpal bones in your wrist.

You will need

Piece of cardboard (the back of a cereal packet would be fine)

Pencil

Sharp pointy scissors

Drinking straws (paper ones work best but plastic ones will do)

PVA glue

String

Wooden skewer (or piece of wire)

Sticky tape

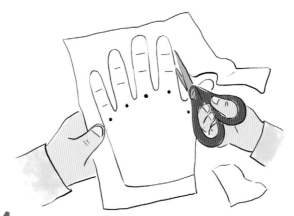

1 Place your hand on the cardboard and draw around it carefully. Mark with a line where your finger and thumb joints are—two in your fingers and one in your thumb. Cut out the hand shape and then fold the cardboard where these lines are and then flatten it again. Put a dot for each of the four knuckle joints at the bottom of your fingers and another dot for the joint at the base of your thumb.

2 Measure and cut off pieces of straw that are the same lengths as your fingers and thumb from tip to knuckle joint. Snip a small triangle shape out of the end of each piece.

WHAT CAN YOU MAKE YOUR HAND DO?

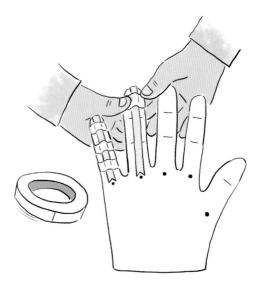

3 Glue the straw pieces onto the cardboard fingers and thumb with the snipped out triangle at the knuckle end and facing up. Secure them more firmly with pieces of sticky tape but don't stick any tape over places where you have marked joints. These straws are like your finger bones or "phalanges."

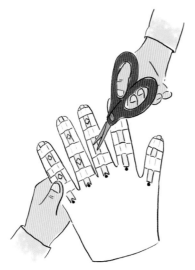

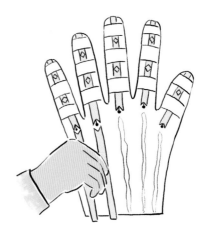

4 Use the scissor points to snip out the top of the straw over all the joints. In your fingers there are separate bones meeting at joints. In the model we cheat and use one straw but make sure it can bend by snipping into it.

5 Cut five more pieces of straw to fit from the bottom knuckles to the wrist for each of the fingers and the thumb. Snip out a triangle shape at one end as before. Glue these pieces to the hand matching up the triangles at the knuckles. Leave the hand to dry. These straws are like your hand bones or "metacarpals."

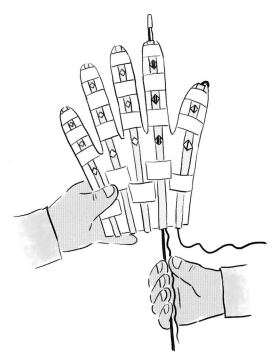

6 Cut five pieces of string each about 9 in. (23 cm) long. You need to thread these through the straws: to make this easier, tape one piece to the end of the skewer or wire and push this up through both the straws to the top of the thumb. Pull the string through (but take care not to pull it too far). Unstick the string from the skewer, and take the end of the string over the top to the other side of the thumb. Secure it with a piece of sticky tape. Do the same for each of the fingers. The string represents the tendons that are attached to your finger bones to make them move.

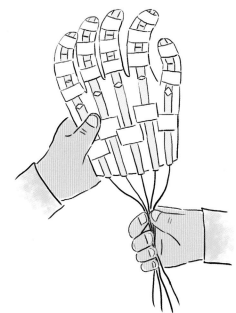

7 Gently pull on each of the strings to make the fingers bend. Can you make your model hand into a fist? In your real hand it is arm muscles that pull the tendons. Try making a fist with your real hand and watch your muscles bulge around your wrist. In your real hand there is a second set of tendons running up the back of your fingers and more muscles that pull on these tendons to straighten your fingers again.

INSIDE THE SCIENCE
One thing the model can't demonstrate is your opposable thumb, which you can touch against any of your fingers on the same hand. An opposable thumb allows you to pick things up and do all kinds of delicate tasks. Try tying your shoe laces, writing your name, picking up a coin, or buttoning a button without using your thumb, to discover just how important it is.

meaty muscles

One muscle bends your arm, one muscle straightens it again. Try making this moving model of your arm to see how a pair of muscles works together.

You will need

Cardboard—a cereal box is fine

Pencil

Scissors

Brad (paper fastener)

Hole punch

String

1 First stand in front of a mirror and bend one arm in a muscle man pose. With the other hand feel the bicep muscle on top of your arm bulge. To straighten your arm again the triceps muscle in the back of your arm has to pull your forearm down. Feel how the bicep stretches and flattens out when you do this.

2 Now cut two bone-shaped pieces from the cardboard—each about 6 in. (15 cm) long and 1 in. (2.5 cm) wide. Your forearm below your elbow is actually two bones—the radius and ulna—so draw a line down the center to show this.

3 Put the lower arm piece down on the table running right to left. Put the upper arm (humerus) piece on top to make an L shape, but about ½ in. (1.5 cm) in from the end of the lower arm piece. Hold the pieces together and push a brad (paper fastener) through both pieces of card where they overlap, to make a hinge—the elbow.

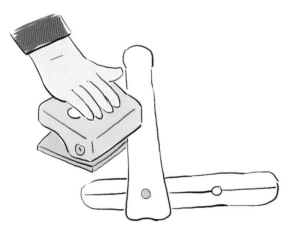

4 Use the hole punch to make one hole about halfway along the lower arm piece. Do the same on the upper arm piece. Thread a piece of string through the hole in the lower arm (with two bones) and knot it so it will not pull through. Thread the other end through the hole in the upper arm, but leave it free. This string is like the bicep muscle. Pull the free end and the arm will bend but you can't straighten it again.

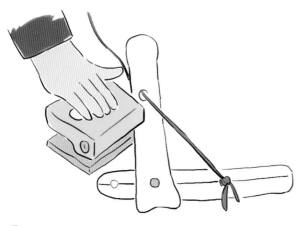

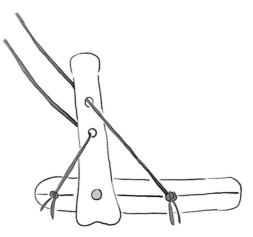

5 Make another hole right at the end of the lower arm piece where it sticks out, by the elbow. Make the last hole between the brad and the hole you have already made in the upper arm.

6 Cut another piece of string, thread it through the hole by the elbow and knot it, and then thread it through the hole in the upper arm and leave it free. This is like your triceps muscle. Hold the upper arm piece, pull this string, and the arm will straighten again!

7 Now sit on a chair and put your hand on your thigh. Straighten out your leg and feel your thigh muscle bulge. Which muscle bends your leg? Flex your foot and you can feel the muscle in your shin bulge. Which muscle do you use to point your toes?

FASCINATING FACT
The jaw muscle is one of the most powerful muscles in the human body. It can produce huge amounts of pressure between your teeth when you bite. Dr G. Black of the Chicago Dental Hospital designed an instrument for measuring the power of the human bite called a gnathodynamometer— learn to say and spell that!

WHO'S THE STRONGEST OF THEM ALL?

make a model of your teeth

The first part of your digestive system is your mouth where your teeth do a very important job—cutting your food into pieces and grinding it up so digestion can begin.

The number of teeth you have in your mouth will depend on how old you are. You only have 20 milk (baby) teeth. When you are about six years old, the first of your adult teeth begin to grow under these and this will make one of your front teeth become wobbly and fall out (with a bit of wiggling help from you). Gradually your milk teeth are replaced with adult teeth and also extra teeth grow— some not until you are 18 years old or older. Adults have 32 teeth and these are called permanent teeth. If you look after them, they will last a lifetime.

1 Roll out two fat sausages of red or pink modeling clay each about 6 in. (15 cm) long and bend them both into C shapes. These represent your upper and lower jaw with the gums over them.

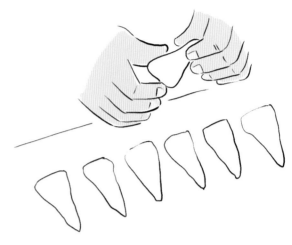

2 Use the mirror to look inside your mouth. First look at your front teeth. These are incisors. They are quite square and thin like a blade. They are used to bite off pieces of your food. Bite a piece of apple to see how you use them. Unless some of your milk teeth have come out, you will have eight incisors—four at the top and four at the bottom. Use white clay (or choose a color) to make eight of these. Each one has a pointed root, which fixes it into your jaw.

3 The next teeth are your canine teeth. These are your pointy vampire teeth, which are used for tearing off food. You have four of them—one at each side, at the top and bottom. Try biting off some crusty bread to see how you use them. Make four canine teeth in white or a different color from the incisors. These also have one root that is extra long because canine teeth need to be strong.

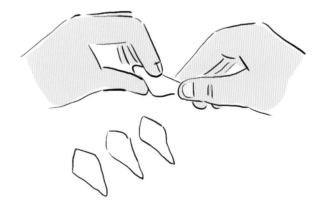

4 The next teeth, depending on your age, are pre-molars and molars. Molars are big, fat, cube-like teeth with four bumps in the corners. They grind together, crushing your food into small pieces—like when you grind up spices in a pestle and mortar. Children have eight molars. You only get pre-molars when you are about 10 years old. They grow next to your canines and are smaller than molars and also have a bumpy surface, as if they have been pushed down in the middle. (Adults have eight pre-molars and six molars.) Count how many molars and pre-molars you have and make that many. Molars have two big pointed roots to hold them in your jaw. Pre-molars only have one.

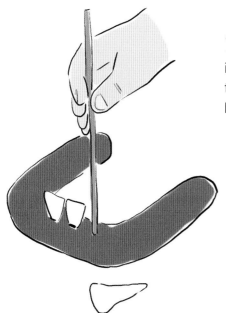

5 Fix each of your teeth into the correct positions in the curved jaw pieces, using the wooden skewer to make holes to drop the root into. Remember to leave gaps if you have teeth missing!

KEEP THOSE TEETH SPARKLING CLEAN!

plaque attack!

Find out how plaque and acid affect your teeth by doing these simple experiments using an eggshell, vinegar, and some disclosing tablets.

You will need

Egg

Saucepan

White vinegar

Small bowl

Slotted spoon

Paper towels

Plaque disclosing tablets (available from drugstores and dentists)

Timer or watch

Toothbrush

Toothpaste

EGG TEST

1 Put an egg into a pan of cold water and ask an adult to help you bring it to the boil. Boil it for about 12 minutes, so that it is solid inside. The eggshell is a bit like the hard enamel of your tooth, protecting the soft egg inside.

2 Carefully take the egg out of the water and put it into the bowl. Pour vinegar into the bowl until the egg is completely covered. We are using vinegar to represent the acid you get on your teeth when you don't clean them. The acid on your teeth comes from the slimy coating called plaque, which is full of bacteria. Every time you eat sugar, the bacteria turn some of it into an acid, like the vinegar.

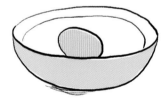

3 Watch the egg in the vinegar. Can you see it is covered in tiny bubbles? These bubbles are carbon dioxide, which is a gas produced when acid reacts with the eggshell. Leave the egg in the vinegar for 48 hours.

4 After 48 hours, lift the egg from the vinegar with the slotted spoon. Put it down on some paper towel and dry it. Now squeeze it and bounce it! The hard shell has become soft. Your teeth will never become soft like this because tooth enamel is much harder than eggshell, but, if you don't brush your teeth, acid from plaque will begin to eat away at the enamel, causing tiny cavities (holes). When there is a hole in the enamel, the softer dentin underneath is eaten away even more quickly to make a bigger cavity. The more often you eat or drink sugary things, the more chance there will be of getting cavities.

TRY THIS
Before you next brush your teeth, check how much plaque you have on them by chewing one of the disclosing tablets. (Follow the instructions on the packet and then look in the mirror.) The tablet contains a dye that stains the plaque bright purple or red. Now brush your teeth and time how long it takes to brush the stained areas clean. However long it takes is the length of time you should brush your teeth for twice a day!

string model of the gut

Have you any idea how long your gut is from your mouth to your anus (the hole in your bottom where poop comes out)? Make this model of your gut with string, rope, and plastic bags and you will find out and be amazed!

You will need

2–3 types of string

Scissors

Small plastic bag

Plastic carrier bag

Thicker rope or string

Sheet of wallpaper or other paper as tall as you are

Friend

Marker pen

Sticky tack or tape

1 Cut a 14–in. (35-cm) piece of string for the esophagus/oesophagus (your throat and the tube to your stomach). Tie one end round the bottom of the small plastic bag so that the plastic bag (your mouth) is only 3 in. (8 cm) long. Trim off the extra bag length.

2 Tie the other end of the "esophagus" to the top of the carrier bag. Tie the string so it ends up 10 in. (25 cm) long. The carrier bag represents your stomach.

YOU'LL BE AMAZED HOW LONG YOUR GUT IS!

3 Cut another piece of string that is 15 ft (4.5 m) long. This really, really long piece is your small intestine. Tie one end around the end of stomach bag so the stomach is 6 in. (15 cm) long. Trim off the extra bag length.

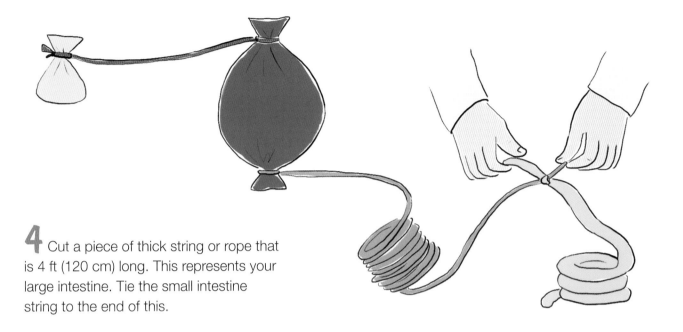

4 Cut a piece of thick string or rope that is 4 ft (120 cm) long. This represents your large intestine. Tie the small intestine string to the end of this.

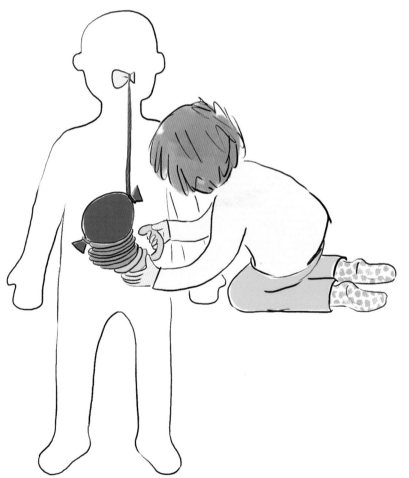

5 Stretch it all out and see just how long it is. Now lie down on the paper and get someone else to draw around you. (If you have made the skeleton drawing on page 110, you already have a body to fit your guts inside!) Find a diagram of your organs online or in a book and arrange the guts inside your body. Use pieces of sticky tack or tape to hold bits in place. The mouth bag will have to go sideways. Can you get it all to fit?

how to make poop!

This is a messy activity guaranteed to disgust you, but it's brilliant fun. It's all about how digestion works and, as everyone knows, digestion ends up with poop.

You will need

Shallow bowl or oven dish

3–4 slices of stale bread

Scissors

Cooked peas, beans, or sweetcorn

Water

Potato masher

Large ziplock food bag

Vinegar

Red and green food coloring

Leg cut from an old pair of pantyhose (tights) with the toe cut off

Large old sock with the toe cut off (optional)

Large plastic bowl

Tray

Paper towels

Friend

Let's begin with the science: you need food for two reasons. First, to give you energy (like a car needs fuel) and second to give you the materials you need to grow, make repairs, and renew bits of yourself throughout your life. The problem here is that the food you eat cannot get to the parts of your body that need it without first being digested. During digestion, food is broken down into nutrients, which can pass into your blood and be transported to every cell of your body.

In this activity (you'll need a friend to help you), you model what happens inside your guts using simple ingredients and equipment from your kitchen. Each step is one of the stages of digestion.

1 When you eat, the first thing you do is to bite off pieces of food—use the scissors instead of your teeth and cut off pieces of bread so that they drop into the shallow bowl. Add a few spoonfuls of peas (or beans or corn) to complete your meal. The bowl represents your mouth.

HEALTH TIPS

Many people think of bacteria as the bad guys who make us ill, but not all bacteria are bad. In fact, bacteria are really important for keeping you healthy. About 500–1,000 different species of bacteria live in your large intestine, munching on any food that gets all the way down there and releasing important chemicals that your body needs, like calcium to make your bones strong and vitamins, which you need to be healthy.

Eat lots of different fruit, vegetables, yogurt, and cheese to make sure you have lots of healthy bacteria inside of you.

Don't be embarrassed to talk about pooping! There is no set number of times you should poop in a week, but if you don't poop very often and it becomes uncomfortable, then it probably means you are constipated. For muscles to squeeze food through a long gut, they need to have something to squeeze against. That's why you need fiber in your diet. Fiber doesn't get digested, but it helps carry everything along and out at the other end.

Fiber is found in food such as fruit and vegetables, baked beans, lentils, whole-wheat cereals, and bread. Eat plenty of these foods and drink plenty of water and pooping should not be a problem, but talk to an adult if it still is.

2 In your mouth, saliva (spit) is mixed with the food so add about half a cup of water to the bowl.

3 Your back teeth (molars) then grind the food into small pieces—use a potato masher for this, mashing everything together until it is a sloppy mess. Add a bit more water if you need to.

4 Next, you swallow and the food passes down your esophagus (oesophagus) into your stomach. The ziplock bag is a model of your stomach so tip everything into the bag. Ask your friend to hold the bag as you do this.

5 In your stomach, acid and enzymes (chemicals) are added that break down the food into nutrients, which can be absorbed into your body. You can add a good shake of vinegar (which is a weak acid) and a few drops each of red and green food coloring. This should make it brown. Zip up the bag to seal it.

6 Your stomach squeezes and mixes the food into a soupy liquid called "chyme." You can use your hands to squeeze and mush the food in the bag until it is all liquid—the peas (or beans or corn) will stay whole.

7 When the food is small enough (after several hours), it is squeezed down into the small intestine, which is a very long tube, coiled up inside you. The leg from the pantyhose (tights) is a model for this. Working together, cut off the bottom corner of the "stomach" bag and squeeze the "chyme" into the pantyhose. Do this over a large bowl.

8 Inside the small intestine, more chemicals are added to the chyme from your pancreas and liver, but you're not doing that. The chyme is pushed along the small intestine by waves of muscle. This is the second type of muscle that you have in your body and is called smooth muscle. Unlike your skeletal muscles, they are controlled automatically by your brain. These muscles begin to work as soon as you swallow so you never have to think about food squeezing through your gut. Show the muscles working by squeezing the top of the pantyhose and pushing the food along with your hands. As it moves, all the food that has been broken down into nutrients passes through the wall of the intestine into the blood stream. You will see some of the liquid drip through the pantyhose into the bowl as it moves along.

9 The remaining food moves on into the large intestine. This is shorter but wider than the small intestine. In here, bacteria break it down some more and our bodies suck out most of the water. Use a sock with the toe cut off for this and squeeze the "chyme" from the pantyhose into the sock. (You could miss out this stage if things are getting messy and just stick with the pantyhose leg.) You can't really model the bacteria working, but we can take out some water. To do this lay some layers of paper towel on the tray, lay the sock on top and roll it up tightly, squeezing as you go. Some of the water will be absorbed by the paper towel.

FASCINATING FACT
You are full of alien life!
It's hard to know how to count them, but scientists estimate that you have roughly the same number of bacteria in your body as you have cells in your body. For an average person, that's more than 30 trillion (30,000,000,000,000) bacteria!

10 And what have you got left? All the things that the body doesn't want or need mixed with some water. Poop! Squeeze it out of the toe of the sock (anus) into the "toilet" (trash can).

make tasty fake blood

Depending on your age and size, you will have between 3½ and 7 pints (2 and 4 liters) of blood in your body—the bigger you grow, the more blood you need. If you cut yourself, you will bleed, but what exactly is blood? It looks like a thick red liquid, but it is made up of four different parts, each with different jobs to do, as you'll discover by doing this activity to make tasty, fruit salad blood!

You will need

⅓ cup (75 g) golden superfine (caster) sugar

⅓ cup (75 g) white superfine (caster) sugar

¾ cup (150 ml) water

Saucepan

1½ cups (200 g) raspberries (big ones if possible)

Straight-sided glass tumbler

1 x 14-oz. (400-g) can of lychees

1 pomegranate

Rolling pin

1 First make some sugar syrup. Put the water and both types of sugar in a pan and ask an adult to help you heat it gently. Stir until the sugar has dissolved. Turn up the heat and bring it to the boil. Turn the heat back down and let it simmer for one minute. Remove from the heat and let it cool.

2 Imagine a disc of modeling clay, which you squeeze between your finger and thumb so there is a dip each side. That's what red blood cells look like, but we're going to use raspberries to represent red blood cells, even though they are not quite the right shape. Cut each raspberry in half and put them in the tumbler to make a thick layer. In your blood, red blood cells carry oxygen to all the other cells in the body. When they are full of oxygen, they are bright red. When the oxygen is used up, they are a darker purple color.

3 Pour the cooled syrup, which should be straw-colored, over the raspberries until the glass contains about half raspberries and half syrup. The syrup represents blood plasma. Just over half (55 percent) of your blood is plasma and this is what makes blood runny.

INSIDE THE SCIENCE
Plasma is mostly water, but it has lots of other things dissolved in it. Plasma's job is to transport nutrients to every cell of the body. It also carries salt and chemical messengers called hormones and it takes away carbon dioxide and other waste from the cells.

4 Open the can of lychees and add 2–3 lychees to the glass. These represent white blood cells.

INSIDE THE SCIENCE
White blood cells are bigger than red cells and there are not nearly so many of them. Their job is to fight infections that try to invade your body.

Platelets make blood clot (become solid) when you cut yourself— otherwise you would just keep bleeding.

If someone cuts themself badly, call for help quickly. Cover the cut with something clean—a clean towel or dish towel if you haven't got a first-aid dressing—and keep pressing firmly on the cut to stop the bleeding. Bleeding stops more quickly if the heart has to pump the blood uphill, so make sure that the cut is held above the person's heart. If the cut is on their arm, get them to hold it up in the air; if it's on their leg, lie them down and raise their leg on a chair, with pillows, if necessary.

You know iron as a metal, but did you know that your body needs iron to make red blood cells. If you don't get enough, you will feel tired and won't have much energy. To get enough, you need to eat foods such as beans, nuts, red meat, eggs, dried fruits (raisins, apricots), and dark green leafy vegetables (cress, spinach, kale). Most breakfast cereals also have iron added to them—does yours?

5 Carefully cut the pomegranate in half (ask an adult to help if it's tough). Lay one half flat on a plate and hit it gently several times with a rolling pin. The seeds should fall out. Add some of the seeds to the mixture. These represent platelets and they are much smaller than red blood cells.

6 Give everything a stir and then put it in the fridge for the flavors to mix before you eat it. If you wanted it to be more like blood, you would warm it up because blood, like the rest of your body, is always the same temperature—about 98.6°F (37°C), but your fruit salad will taste nicer cold!

WHAT'S ON THE MENU?

find out about your heart

Your heart is a pump that never stops pumping blood around your body. These simple activities will help you learn more about how it works. You will even be able to hear your own heartbeat, like a doctor does!

You will need

Small funnel

Piece of plastic tube or hosepipe about 18 in. (46 cm) long

Strong sticky tape

Scissors

Old tennis ball

MAKE A STETHOSCOPE

1 Push the plastic tube inside the tube of the funnel (or the funnel inside the tube if the tube is wider). Secure it tightly with sticky tape wrapped several times around it so there are no gaps.

2 Hold the funnel against your skin on the left side of your chest, where your heart is, and hold the end of the tube against your ear. Listen to your heartbeat. Move the funnel around until you can hear it clearly. The "lub-dub, lub-dub" heartbeat sound you can hear is the sound of the heart valves snapping shut. They don't shut at quite the same time, which is why you hear the double sound.

LUB-DUB, LUB-DUB, LUB-DUB!

INSIDE THE SCIENCE
Your heart has two sides and each side is divided into two parts with valves between them (like doors), which open and shut as the blood moves from one to the other. When the body has used up oxygen from the blood it flows into the top of the right side of your heart, it is squeezed into the bottom of your heart, and then shoots off to the lungs. It comes back to the top left full of oxygen, is squeezed into the bottom of the heart and an extra big squeeze shoots it off around the body. The more exercise you do, the more energy your body needs and so the faster the blood has to pump around your body bringing it oxygen and nutrients.

3 Use a timer and count how many times your heart beats in 15 seconds. Double this number and double again to find your heart rate for 1 minute. Now jump or dance around for 5 minutes then listen and count again. Work out your new heart rate. (Or you could use a heart rate app on a phone—there are lots of free ones available.) Every beat is a squeeze that shoots blood out and around your body or to your lungs.

HOW DOES YOUR HEART WORK?

1 Now try something else. Carefully, use the point of a sharp pair of scissors to pierce a hole in the tennis ball (ask an adult to help you). Push the scissors right in and twist them around to make the hole a bit bigger.

2 Fill your sink with water. Squeeze the ball to push out as much air as possible and then dunk it in the sink so that it fills up with water. Take it out of the water. Keeping it over the sink, squeeze the ball hard. The water will shoot out. Keep squeezing as you put it back in the water, then relax your squeeze and it will fill up again. This is how your heart works—it squeezes to push blood out and relaxes to let blood in. Empty the tennis ball.

3 Now hold it with your arm stretched out at shoulder height. Pretend your hand is a heart that has to keep squeezing the tennis ball every second (the tennis ball is a just a bit bigger than your heart, which is about the same size as your fist). How quickly do the muscles in your hand get tired? After 20 squeezes, 50 squeezes, 100 squeezes?

If your pulse rate is 80 beats a minute, your heart beats about 4,800 times in an hour, or 42,048,000 (that's more than 42 million) times in a year—and never gets tired. This shows how different and special your heart muscles are.

make a model of your lungs

Take some really big breaths to fill your lungs with air. You can make a model of your lungs to find out how they work.

You will need

Plastic bottle with a lid

Sharp scissors

Two balloons

Sticky parcel tape

Hand drill (optional)

Drinking straw

Sticky tack

Small elastic band

When you breathe in, imagine the air rushing in through your nose and down the tube (trachea) at the back of your throat. There the tube splits into two smaller tubes, one going to each lung. These tubes branch into even smaller tubes, so each lung looks a bit like an upside-down tree. The smallest branches end with tiny air sacs which are covered in tiny blood capillaries. Blood is pumped to the lung by the heart when it is full of carbon dioxide and almost empty of oxygen. The carbon dioxide moves out of the blood into the lung and you breathe it out. When you breathe in again, air fills the lungs and the oxygen from the air moves into the blood. The blood, now full of oxygen, travels to your heart to be pumped around your body.

1 Carefully cut the bottom off the plastic bottle—ask an adult to help you.

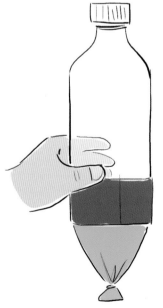

2 Tie a knot in the neck of one of the balloons. Cut open the bottom and then stretch the balloon across the open base of the bottle. It should be very tight. Secure it with strong sticky tape.

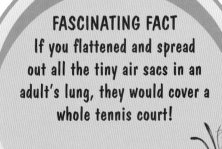

FASCINATING FACT
If you flattened and spread out all the tiny air sacs in an adult's lung, they would cover a whole tennis court!

3 Make a hole in the bottle lid. You may need to ask an adult to help you with this—you can do it with pointy scissors, but using a hand drill is an easier way. The hole needs to be just big enough to push the straw through. Cut a piece of straw about 4 in. (10 cm) long and push it half through the lid. Mold some sticky tack around the hole to make an airtight seal.

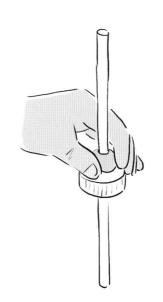

4 Blow up the second balloon and then let the air out again (to make it easy to blow up again). Use an elastic band to attach the balloon to the straw below the lid. Twist the elastic over several times so that it is very tight. Push the balloon into the bottle and screw on the lid.

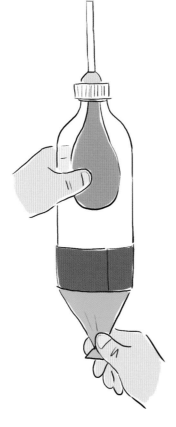

5 Gently pull on the balloon at the base of the bottle and you should see the balloon inside the bottle inflate.

INSIDE THE SCIENCE
Below your lungs you have a big muscle called the diaphragm, which is stretched across your chest. When it is relaxed, it is a dome shape, but when you breathe in, it flattens, pulling down just like the balloon. This makes a bigger space in your lungs. At the same time your ribs move up and out, making an even bigger space. Air rushes into your lungs to even out the pressure; in other words, you breathe in. Then the diaphragm relaxes and goes back to a dome shape, your ribs drop back, the pressure in the lungs increases, and the air rushes out—you breathe out.

6 Pulling the balloon down makes a bigger space inside the bottle for the same amount of air, so the air pressure is lower. Air outside the bottle tries to get in to even out the pressure but it can only get into the balloon, so the balloon inflates. The same thing happens inside your chest.

test your lungs

Your lungs will grow as you grow. The amount of air your lungs hold also increases when you are very fit, so there is no set amount for how much air your lungs will hold but it's fun to find out. This is easier to do with a friend.

You will need

- 2-quart (2-liter) drinks bottle with a lid
- Length of plastic tubing
- Measuring pitcher (jug)

1 Fill the bottle with water right to the very top and screw on the lid. Fill your sink with water until it is about 6 in. (14 cm) deep. Turn the bottle over and, with the top underwater, unscrew the lid. Get your friend to hold it upright.

2 Keeping the bottle top under the water, push one end of the tube inside the bottle. Breathe in deeply and blow into the other end of the tube for as long as you can, until there is no air left in your lungs. All the air you breathe out will bubble to the top of the bottle.

3 Still keeping the top underwater, screw the cap back onto the bottle. Lift it out and turn it over. The amount of air in the bottle is the same as the amount of air you breathed out of your lungs. If you want to know the capacity of your lungs in fluid ounces (milliliters), pour the water that is left in the bottle into a measuring pitcher (jug) and measure how much there is. Subtract this amount from the amount that the bottle originally contained (2 quarts/liters) and you have your lung capacity. Now wash the tube and let your friend have a go.

making snot!

To understand more about what snot is (and to gross out your friends), make some fake snot and then find out why you should never sneeze into your hand.

You will need

Kettle

2 small bowls

3 packets of unflavored gelatin

Fork

¼ cup (4 tablespoons) corn (golden) syrup

Green food coloring

Vaseline

Glitter

1 Ask an adult to help you heat water in a kettle until it is very hot, but not quite boiling. Pour half a cup of the almost boiling water into a bowl and sprinkle on the three packets of gelatine. Stir the powder in with a fork and then leave to soften for 5 minutes.

2 Put the corn (golden) syrup into another bowl.

3 Stir the gelatin mix with a fork until all the lumps have gone and then slowly add it to the corn syrup until your mixture looks like snot. Use a fork to stir it, as it will pull out long strands of snot. Add a few drops of green food coloring to make it even more disgusting. This looks like snot because it is made of the same ingredients as snot—protein, sugar, and water. They are different types of protein and sugar, but snot has a very similar chemical make-up.

4 Now wipe a very thin smear of Vaseline onto a door handle that everyone in your family uses a lot. Sprinkle a thin layer of glitter all over it—it should stick to the Vaseline. Don't tell anyone.

5 After a while get everyone to check their hands to see if there is glitter on them. Become a detective and check other places to find how far the glitter has spread. Imagine that you had cold and had sneezed into your hand and then opened a door. The bacteria and viruses from your snot would have been wiped onto the door handle. The next person who opened the door would have got it on their hands and spread it further and probably caught your cold. This is why you should never sneeze into your hand— unless you are going to wash it straight away!

make a brain hat

Make a brain hat to show which area of the very top layer of your brain—your cerebral cortex—does what. Then, for instance, when you speak, you can point (using the power of several other areas of your brain) and say, "This part is working now!"

You will need

Large round balloon

Newspaper

White PVA glue

2 small bowls

White paper (recycle old computer printouts)

Pencil

Acrylic paints

Paintbrushes

Black marker pens

Some people say that one side of your brain can be more in control than the other. Those whose left side is more in control are supposed to be good at mathematics and science, and those whose right side is more in control are supposed to be good at creative subjects, such as art and music. But this is a myth! Don't let anyone tell you that your brain only allows you to be good at one of these areas. However, the left side does control and sense the right side of your body and the right side controls and senses the left side of your body.

Of course, most of your brain is underneath the cerebral cortex and that keeps working all the time too. The brain hat is only a guide to what is going on, but it's cool to make and wear.

1 Prepare a messy area—spread out some sheets of newspaper to protect the work surface and put on an apron.

HEALTH TIPS
Your skull does a good job of protecting your brain, but you still need to take good care of it yourself. Always wear a properly fitted helmet for activities like cycling, horse riding, skateboarding, skiing, or anything else where you risk banging your head.

2 Blow up the balloon so it is as big as your head. Place it on top of a small bowl, tied end down, to hold it steady.

3 Pour some PVA glue into the other bowl and mix in about the same amount of water to thin it. Tear some newspaper into strips, and then tear the strips into rough pieces about 1½ in. (4 cm) square.

4 Dip a square into the glue and then stick it down on the balloon. Keep going, dipping and sticking, overlapping each square with the next. You only need cover the balloon down to its widest point to make a hat.

5 Stick two layers of newspaper pieces over the balloon. Now tear up and dip the white paper and cover the newspaper layers with one layer of white paper. Smooth it down with your hands. Leave in a warm place to dry out completely.

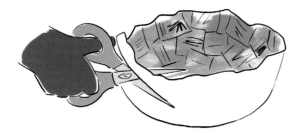

6 Pop the balloon and remove it from inside the hat. Trim the edge with scissors to neaten it and try it for size.

7 Use a pencil to divide the hat into two halves down the middle— these will represent the left side and right side of your brain. Now mark out the areas on the brain as shown in the diagrams opposite. Paint the areas using the same four colors that we have used—not too dark as you need to write on them afterward.

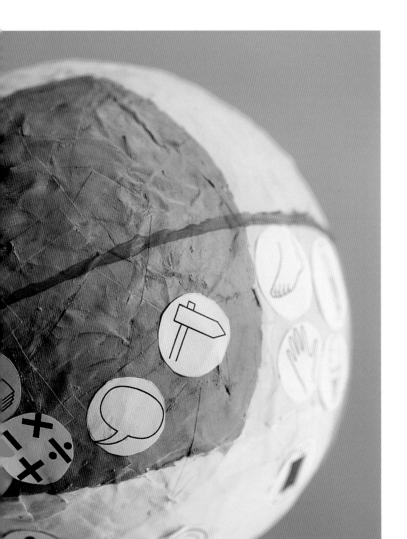

8 When the hat is dry, use marker pens to label each area on the right side of the brain hat with its correct name following this key:

pink = frontal lobe
green = parietal lobe
blue = occipital lobe
yellow = temporal lobe

Remember that the pink frontal lobe is the front of the hat.

9 Now photocopy the symbols (right) and cut them out. Stick the symbols for what each area does on the left side of the brain, following the diagram for the left side of the brain.

Top diagram

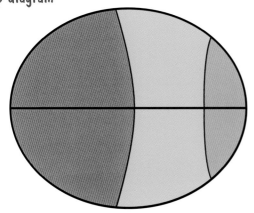

Right diagram

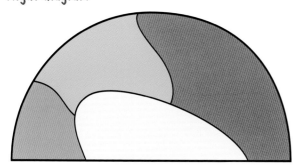

Left diagram

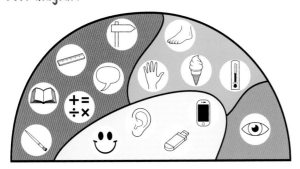

KEY TO SYMBOLS

Eye movement (understanding where you are)

Speech

Planning

Reasoning and calculating

Concentrating

Creativity

Emotion

Hearing

Memory

Understanding language

Sight and understanding what you see

Movement

Taste

Temperature

Touch

billions of connections

You have billions of neurons in your brain and nervous system and each neuron connects with other neurons. Every time you learn something or remember something, more connections are made between different neurons in your brain.

You will need

Either:

Small piece of stiff card

Ruler and pencil

2-hole punch

Blunt needle with a big eye

Lots of different colored yarns

Sticky tape

Scissors

Or:

Paper

Ruler

Colored pencils or fine pens

A hundred billion is the number of neurons that scientists estimate you have in your brain and you can multiply that number by millions more to find out the number of connections.
Even with just a few connections, things quickly get complicated as you can see with this activity.
You can do it in two ways: you can either use a needle and colored yarn to join holes in the card or join the dots with colored pencils and a ruler. Imagine the dots are neurons. The colored yarns or lines are connections. Both look pretty impressive.

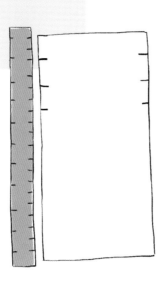

1 Cut a rectangle of card about 4 in. (10 cm) wide and 8 in. (20 cm) long. Use a ruler and make a mark every ¾ in. (2 cm) down each side. Join up the first four pairs of marks across the card.

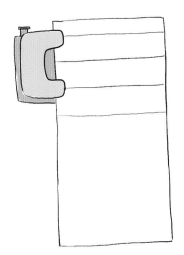

2 Push on the hole punch so the edge is against the first pencil line. Punch two holes. Move the hole punch along and line it up with the next pencil line and punch two more holes. Do this twice more and you will have eight evenly spaced holes. Now do the same on the opposite edge of the card so that there are another eight holes along this side. Turn the card over so the unmarked side is on top.

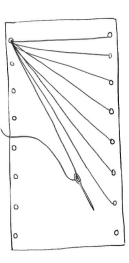

3 Thread the needle with a piece of colored yarn about 68 in. (170 cm) long. Tape the end to the back of your card. Bring the needle up through the first hole on the left side and then down through the first hole on the right side, then back up where you started and down the second hole on the right side. Keep going until you have connections from the first hole on the left to all the holes on the right. Finish on the back, take off the needle, cut off the extra yarn, and secure the end with sticky tape. Each line of yarn represents a connection of one neuron with another.

FASCINATING FACT
It is easier for your brain to make neural connections when you are young than when you are older, so now is the time to learn difficult skills such as playing a musical instrument or learning a language. When you learn something new, neural pathways are set up in your brain and in time that activity becomes automatic— you can do it without thinking.

FASCINATING FACT

Some neurons are several feet (meters) long! Other cells in your body are always being replaced but neurons must last you a lifetime. However, some get destroyed and you will end up with fewer neurons when you are old than you have now.

4 Choose the next color and repeat the process connecting the second hole on the left side with all the holes on the right side. Continue until all eight holes are connected with each other. You will have 64 connections and a cool piece of embroidery! Now try to imagine the connections if you had billions of holes down each side!

VARIATION

If you prefer to draw rather than sew, do almost the same. Measure and draw dots every ¾ in. (2 cm) all down each side and use a ruler and different colors to join each dot on the left side to all the dots on the right side. It soon gets complicated! Just imagine what is going on inside your brain!

CHAPTER FOUR
outside science

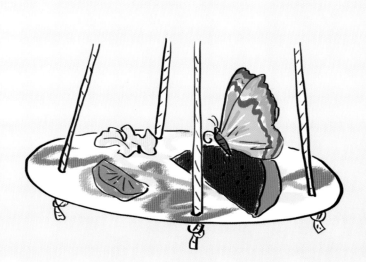

we're going on a seed hunt

Plants need to produce seeds so new plants can grow. Seeds come in all sorts of shapes and sizes and they have all kinds of crazy ways to try to get to a new place to grow. This is called dispersal. Why not go on a seed hunt to find seeds that are dispersed in different ways?

You will need

Fine day in late summer or fall (autumn)

Some egg cartons with lids

Backpack to carry them in

1 On a fine day in late summer or fall (autumn), set off on your seed hunt with your egg cartons in a backpack so that your hands are free. Your seed hunt could be around your backyard or you could ask an adult to take you to woods, fields, or a park. Everywhere you go you will find seeds of all shapes and sizes inside seed cases of all shapes and sizes. Try to collect different types in the compartments of your egg cartons. Keep the cartons upright in your pack!

SAFETY FIRST
Always wash your hands after you have been exploring outside.

2 Find seeds like dandelions, with feather-light parachutes. These are blown around by the wind. Blow some from a plant and see how far they go.

3 Find a winged seed with a helicopter action— sycamore or maple trees have these. As they fall from the trees they spin. This means they take longer to fall and so the wind has more chance to catch them and whisk them to somewhere new. Stretch up high and drop a handful to see them spin.

WHICH SEEDS CAN FLY?

4 Find seeds that stick to your clothes or your dog's fur. Look at each one closely and you will see it is covered in tiny hooks. When you or an animal shakes one off it will fall in a different place.

5 Find a pepper pot! Poppy seeds come in "pepper pots." When they dry, their seed cases have tiny holes around the top. The wind blows, shaking the pot, and the tiny seeds are shaken out.

6 Find some nuts. Nuts have hard shells inside an outer covering, which can be quite thin like a hazelnut, or prickly like chestnuts. Squirrels love nuts and they bury them to eat in the winter but they often forget where they have put some of them. These can grow into new trees.

7 Find some blackberries and look for purple bird poop nearby. Birds love juicy berries but the seeds inside the berries go right through them and come out the other end. The seed starts to grow in its own little pile of manure.

8 Find some pine cones whose woody scales are open. Shake the seeds out. The scales only open when the seeds are ripe and then they can shake out in the wind. Some pine seeds have wings so they can blow farther in the wind.

9 Find some seeds that grow in pods like peas. When the pods dry they split open suddenly and the seeds shoot out.

10 You may be lucky and find some other exploding seed cases. You can hear these pop and the seeds might even hit you. They usually explode in the sun on hot days when their seed pods dry out or when you touch them.

11 What is the biggest seed you can find and what is the smallest?

INSIDE THE SCIENCE

To grow well, seeds need to find some good soil with enough water, light, and space around them. If they all just drop off their parent plant, they will all be trying to grow in one place——it will be too crowded and the parent plant will take all the nutrients. So the plant tries to disperse its seeds as widely as possible. Plants may produce thousands of seeds but only a very few land in the perfect spot and grow into a new plant.

a pitfall trap

You have probably read stories in which animals are trapped when they fall into holes disguised by branches and leaves. A pitfall trap is just like that but smaller. By setting one up in your backyard, you will be able to catch and investigate some of the fascinating bugs that scuttle around on the ground when you're not looking!

You will need

Trowel

Coffee or baby formula can—or any other metal can with a plastic top

Piece of wooden board or a tile that is bigger than the can

Four pebbles or stones—all about the same size

Tray with steep sides or a wide shallow box

White paper

Bug pot with a magnifying lens, or a magnifying glass

Book to help you identify your catches (optional)

Notebook and pencil

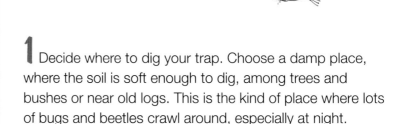

SAFETY FIRST
Always wash your hands after you have been exploring outside.

1 Decide where to dig your trap. Choose a damp place, where the soil is soft enough to dig, among trees and bushes or near old logs. This is the kind of place where lots of bugs and beetles crawl around, especially at night.

2 Dig a hole as big as the can and put your can into it. Fill up any gaps around the can with loose soil so that the can fits snugly in the hole with the rim just below soil level. If there is any rim showing above the soil the bugs will simply walk around the rim!

3 Make sure the ground around the pot is a place where bugs would like to be—smooth it down and put back any sticks, stones, and leaf litter (leaves that have been rotting since last year), which you may have pushed out of the way. Put a little damp leaf litter in the bottom of the can so your captives are comfortable.

4 Put the board over the top of the can and then place a stone under each corner to hold the board just above the ground. This way the bugs will crawl under the board and fall into the trap. It will be cool and shady underneath in the daytime and the board will also keep out rain.

5 Leave the trap for 24 hours. Before you check it, cover the bottom of the tray or box with white paper. Then, take out the can and tip your catch into the tray. Be careful not to let any captives escape—some beetles move very quickly! The bugs will show up clearly on the white surface. See how many different bugs you have caught.

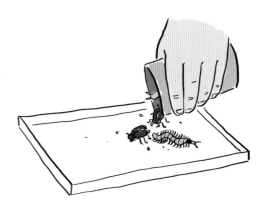

6 Use the bug pot or magnifying glass to examine each one more closely. How many can you identify? A good scientist will record what they have found in a notebook.

TRAP YOURSELF A WILD BEASTIE!

7 Once you have had a good look, put all the bugs and beetles back on the ground, near the trap.

8 You might want to set up the trap just once, in which case fill the hole back up with soil. If you want to try several times, put the can back but you must check it every 24 hours so that creatures (including small frogs and toads) don't get left in the trap with no food or water. If you are not going to be able check it, or if it is going to rain hard (which could drown your captives) put the lid on the can. You can take it off again when you next want to use the trap.

INSIDE THE SCIENCE

The correct name for a bug is an invertebrate, which means an animal without a backbone. Invertebrates have no skeletons inside their bodies but may have a hard outside called an exoskeleton. Spiders and insects have exoskeletons but slugs and worms have no hard parts at all. There may be hundreds of different invertebrates scuttling or creeping around your yard, especially at night. Even though many are good climbers, if they fall into your trap their feet will not be able to grip on the smooth wall of the coffee can so they will be trapped.

get to know a tree

Scientists who study plants and animals often need to watch them for a long time to see how they change or what happens to them in different seasons. The other projects in this book are mostly pretty quick but this one is all about taking time. Take time to get to know a tree because trees are amazing. If you really want to be a scientist, see if you have the sticking power to record what happens to a favorite tree over a whole year. Take photos, write notes, draw pictures, and end up with a really special diary.

SAFETY FIRST
Always wash your hands after you have been exploring outside.

You will need

A favorite tree

Tree identification guide

Special notebook

Pencil

Blindfold

Wax crayon

Paper—thin is best

Camera and printer

Glue stick

Teaspoon

Bug pot

1 Choose a tree Choose one in your backyard or nearby in a park or in the wild. Choose one you think is special perhaps because of its shape or because it's really tall, or even better because it has a few low branches so that you can climb it. A deciduous tree is one that loses its leaves in the fall (autumn) and is probably more interesting than an evergreen because there will be more changes to record. Identify your tree by using your guide. This is easier in the summer when the trees have their leaves. Look at the shape and size of the tree, the shape of its leaves, and what sort of seeds it has to help you find what type of tree it is.

2 Hug your tree

If there are a few other trees near to your tree this is a fun activity, but you will need someone to help you. Start by looking at your tree really carefully. Look at where the lowest branches are. Look at how wide the trunk it. Look at how rough the bark is and any special marks on it. Ask the other person to blindfold you, to turn you around a few times so you don't know where you are, then to lead you to a tree. Now you need to hug the tree, to feel it all over and to try and decide whether or not it is your chosen tree! If it isn't your tree, get the other person to take you to your tree so you can hug it and get to know it through touch. Write a few words about it in your notebook.

3 Make bark and leaf rubbings

Peel the paper off a wax crayon. Hold a piece of paper against the tree trunk and rub over it with the side of the crayon. You will see the pattern of the bark on the paper. Do some leaf rubbings in a similar way. Put a leaf on a table with the veiny side up. Cover it with paper and rub with the side of the wax crayon. Neatly cut out the best section of bark rubbing and the best leaf rubbings and stick them in your notebook.

HUG A TREE TODAY

4 **Start your tree diary** Try to notice your tree every day as you walk to school or play in your backyard. Watch for changes each season brings and record them in your notebook. Look for these changes: When do the leaves start to change color? When in the fall (autumn) are they most colorful? When are there no leaves left? When does the first leaf bud split open in spring? When are all the leaves fully open? When do you see the first flowers and what do they look like? (Yes, trees have flowers too!) When do the nuts, berries, or other type of seeds look ripe and ready for squirrels or birds to eat? What does your tree look like in the snow? Has your tree lost any branches in a storm? Each time you see a change in your tree, take a photo and stick it in your diary with the date and a few notes.

5 **Do a wildlife survey** Search all around your tree for the creatures that live there. Dig around the roots for beetles and worms. Check all the nooks and crannies in the bark for spiders, snails, and other bugs. Check leaves for caterpillars. Use the teaspoon to catch interesting bugs in your bug pot for a closer look but remember to let them go again. Sit under your tree, or in a branch if it is safe to climb, and watch to see if birds or other animals visit your tree. Make a list of everything you see there.

6 **Visit your tree at night** Ask an adult to take you to watch your tree on a clear night. Listen to the sounds around your tree at night. There may be owls out hunting or bats flying around. In winter try taking a photo of the moon through the branches.

INSIDE THE SCIENCE
See if you can find out more about how amazing trees are and how much we need them. Trees give us shade, shelter, wood to build, fuel for fires, fruit and nuts to eat. They take carbon dioxide out of the atmosphere and put back oxygen, which we need to breathe. Their leaves turn into soil to grow our food and their roots stop soil from being washed away. They are also home to many, many other creatures.

stop-motion bean pot

Have you ever wondered what happens to seeds after you've planted them in the ground? Now you can find out with these stop-motion bean pots. They will show you the stages of germination and you will be rewarded with a bean plant ready to put in the garden.

You will need

Cardboard tube

Newspaper

Sticky tape

Potting mix (compost)

Clear plastic pint-sized beaker

Colored paper napkins

Pole/Runner or green (climbing French) bean seeds. Instead of runner beans you could grow other types of beans—French beans, fava (broad) beans, or borlotti beans. Only climbing beans will need a cane for support

Small pitcher (jug)

Hand trowel

Bamboo cane

Watering can

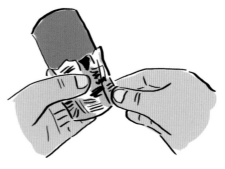

1 Place the cardboard tube end down on a double layer of newspaper. Now gather up the newspaper around the tube and secure it with sticky tape. It doesn't have to be neat but one end of the tube must be sealed.

2 Carefully fill the tube with some potting mix (compost), making sure that you firm it down inside the tube as you go (but don't push it through the paper end!). Place the tube in the plastic beaker and stuff paper napkins in the space between the tube and the sides of the beaker.

WATCH HOW SEEDS GROW!

3 Use your finger to make a hole about 1½ in. (4 cm) deep in the potting mix. Plant a bean seed in the hole, cover it over with more potting mix, and then firm it down. Try not to spill any over the side of the tube.

4 Push another bean seed about 1½ in. (4 cm) down the side of the beaker between the beaker and the napkin so that you can see it clearly from the outside.

5 With a small pitcher (jug), slowly add water to the tube and beaker so that the potting mix and napkins are both damp.

6 After two days, push another bean down the side of the beaker but a little farther along. Keep doing this every two days until you have 6–8 seeds around your pot. Keep the potting mix and napkins damp. Watch the beans begin to germinate one by one and then, as you turn the beaker around, you will be able to see the whole germination process unfold from start to finish.

7 When the central bean has grown two large leaves and you are certain that there will be no more frosts, take the whole cardboard tube carefully out of the beaker. Find a warm sunny spot in your yard, dig a hole that is as deep as the tube, and place the tube into it. Fill the hole with soil around the tube and firm it down with your hands. The tube will rot away as the bean grows. Water it well.

INSIDE THE SCIENCE

Seeds come in all different shapes and sizes but inside every seed is a tiny plant (called an embryo) and a store of food. The hard outside, called the seed case, protects the embryo and stops it drying out. The seed stays dormant (which means it doesn't grow) until it has the right amount of water, air, and warmth. Then the seed case splits and the embryo uses the food store to begin growing. A root grows first, then a shoot, and then the first leaves appear. As soon as the plant has green leaves it can begin to make its own food by photosynthesis (see page 175).

8 Push a garden cane into the soil beside the bean plant—the plant will twine itself around the cane as it grows, but you might want to help it to start climbing by tying it to the cane. Remember, beans are thirsty plants so keep it well watered.

nature's color palette

A color palette is what artists use to paint a picture. They begin with a few colors and mix them to make many more. Look around you when you are out in your backyard or in the countryside or a park. Nature uses hundreds of different colors in its color palette. In this project you will collect tiny samples of different leaves or flower petals to investigate.

You will need

Cardboard

Pencil

Ruler

Scissors

Double-sided sticky tape

SAFETY FIRST
Always wash your hands after you have been exploring outside.

1 Cut the cardboard into small rectangles about 4 x 2 in. (10 x 5 cm) but don't worry too much about exact sizes as it doesn't really matter too much.

2 Stick rows of double-sided sticky tape to one side of a piece of cardboard so that it is completely covered.

3 Take your cardboard outside and pull the paper backing off the tape to leave a sticky surface (this can be a bit tricky).

A COLOR MOSAIC

4 Decide what you want to investigate. In the fall (autumn) you might want to look at leaf colors. Tear off tiny pieces of leaves about the size of your little fingernail. Start with all the yellows you can find and stick each one to your piece of cardboard. Move into oranges, then reds, then browns so that you have a spectrum of different colors. Cover every space on your cardboard with a mosaic of different-colored leaf pieces.

5 In the spring or summer you could use flower petals instead. One of you could search for pink and red flowers while someone else searches for yellow and orange and someone else for blue and purple—or you could mix all the colors up together. If you only take a fingernail-sized sample of a flower you won't damage it. Never pick whole flowers because then you will be stealing the nectar from the bees and you will stop that flower from making seeds.

INSIDE THE SCIENCE

Inside a leaf are three different color chemicals—one is green, one is yellow, and one is orange. In the summer the green chemical, called chlorophyll, does a very important job. Along with sunlight, water, and carbon dioxide from the air, chlorophyll makes food for the plant in a process called photosynthesis. While this is going on the green color is very strong and hides the other colors. But plants need sunlight to create chlorophyll—without it they turn yellow. With less sun in the fall (autumn), there is less chlorophyll, the green fades, and the yellow and orange colors can be seen. Then as the weather begins to get colder, a layer of cork-like cells grows across the leaf stalks ready for when the leaves fall from the trees. Chemicals are trapped in the leaves and these react with sunlight and turn red.

Flowers are colorful to attract insects (or sometimes even birds or animals). An insect, such as a bee, will settle on a flower to sip nectar from it. While it is visiting, pollen sticks to its body, then the bee flies off in search of more food. It settles on a new flower and the pollen from the last flower rubs off onto the new one. Pollen is needed by the flower to make seeds so the flowers are brightly colored to attract the flying pollinators. Bees are especially attracted to bright blue and violet colors. Hummingbirds prefer red, pink, fuchsia, or purple flowers. Butterflies enjoy bright colors such as yellow, orange, pink, and red.

brilliant butterflies

Not everyone likes insects or bugs but everyone loves butterflies. It is one of the loveliest sights on a summer day to see butterflies fluttering from flower to flower, sipping nectar. The best way to get butterflies to visit your garden is to plant their favorite flowers but you can also make one of these easy-peasy butterfly feeders and a special insect watering hole. Put them both out in your backyard on a sunny day in summer and see who comes to visit.

You will need

- Ruler
- Paper plate
- Pencil
- Sharp pointy scissors
- Colored pens or pencils
- String
- Mushy, ripe fruit
- Saucer/tray from under a plant pot
- Some small flat pebbles
- Pitcher (jug) or watering can

1 First make the butterfly feeder. Place your ruler across the center of the plate and draw a very faint line. Draw a dot at each end ½ in. (1 cm) from the edge of the plate. Turn the ruler and draw another line at right angles to the first one so it makes a cross. Put dots ½ in. (1 cm) from the ends of this line too.

2 Use the point of a pair of sharp scissors to make a hole where you have put each of the four dots.

3 Butterflies prefer white, pink, purple, red, yellow, and orange flowers so decorate your plate in some of these colors. If you want to be a real scientist, make several feeders in different colors and see which the butterflies prefer.

4 Cut four pieces of string each about 11 in. (28 cm) long. Tie a big knot in the end of each piece and thread the other end through each of your four holes.

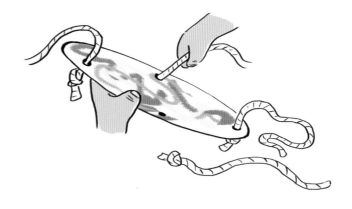

5 Tie the four pieces together so the plate hangs level like an upside-down parachute.

6 Hang it near some flowers and put some small pieces of mushy fruit onto it. Butterflies really love those mushy bananas that no one else will eat!

FIX UP A BUTTERFLY FEAST

TIP
On hot days remember to keep topping up the water in your watering hole so it doesn't dry up.

7 Now for the watering hole. Place the saucer on the ground near your feeder and fill it with a layer of small flat pebbles.

8 Pour water into the tray until it fills the spaces between the stones. The water should not cover the stones. These are for the butterflies to land on.

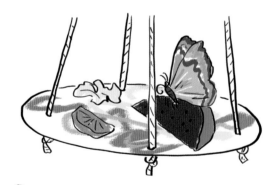

9 Watch to see how many butterflies or other insects visit your feeder or land in your watering hole for a sip of water.

INSIDE THE SCIENCE

Butterflies do not eat; they only suck up liquids with their proboscis, which is a long tube and acts like a straw. When they are not feeding, the proboscis is curled up under their head. (Look out for it on the butterflies that land on your feeder.) They use it to suck nectar out of flowers but also to suck up fruit juice, water, and other liquids. They do not taste with their mouths but with their feet, which have taste sensors on them.

color change flowers

Begin with some plain white carnations and change them into any color you like—even multicolored. And it's all because of science, not magic.

You will need

4 glass jars or 4 glasses

Water

Food coloring in 4 different colors

6 white carnations, or other white flowers with strong stems

Cutting board

Sharp knife (ask an adult to help you)

1 Half-fill all the glass jars with water. Add a different food coloring to each jar. Keep adding drops until the water is a strong color—you'll probably need to add 20–30 drops.

2 Ask an adult to help you. Lay one flower on the cutting board and cut off the end of the stem at a slight diagonal. Do the same with all the flowers.

TURN A WHITE FLOWER BLUE

3 Put one flower in each of the four jars and place them on a bright, sunny windowsill. Push them close together so the jars are touching each other in a line.

4 This next part is a bit tricky and it is easy to cut your fingers, so ask an adult to do it for you. They need to slit the stems of the other two flowers up the middle, but not quite all the way to the top. Stop a couple of inches (about 5 cm) from the head of the flower. Pull the two halves of each stem gently apart.

5 Place the split stems so that one half is in one jar and the other half in the jar next to it. You should end up with one flower with half a stem in the red water and half a stem in the blue water, and the other flower with half a stem in the yellow water and half a stem in the green water.

6 Leave the flowers for 4–6 hours. Keep checking as gradually the flowers change color! What happens to the flowers with the split stems?

INSIDE THE SCIENCE

The flowers have a network of tiny tubes in them taking water and food to every cell in the plant. In bright sunlight, water evaporates from the flower petals. This means that more water is sucked up into the tiny tubes that run up the stem. The stem would normally be attached to roots, which would suck up water from the soil but, in this project, the ends of the stems are in the colored water and so this is sucked up into the tubes. As more water evaporates from the flowers the colored water is gradually drawn up through the stems and into the flowers, turning them different colors. The flowers with the split stems will be colored half and half. The red mixed with blue will be half red, half blue, and the yellow mixed with green will be half yellow, half green!

worm charming

You have probably heard of snake charming but have you ever heard of worm charming? Did you know that there is even a *World Worm Charming Championship?* The point of worm charming is to make as many worms as possible come up out of the ground. This project is a lot of fun, especially if you make it into a competition with some friends.

You will need

Lawn or field

4 tent pegs or garden skewers for each competitor

Ball of string

Small bucket for each competitor with a covering cloth or lid

Some garden forks and spades

Timer

Big sticks

Musical instruments

Ruler

Weighing scales

Magnifying glass

Prizes or homemade certificates

1 First, mark out a plot for each competitor that is about 2 x 2 big paces. Push in a tent peg for one corner of a plot. Take two big paces and push in another tent peg. Turn a corner and take two more paces for the third corner. Keep going to make a square. Stretch string around the tent pegs.

2 Either choose which plot you want (think—where would worms most like to live?) or number the plots and draw numbers out of a hat to choose who has each one. Put a layer of damp soil in each bucket and find a cloth or lid to cover the bucket with.

WHERE ARE YOU, WORMS?!

3 The world championship gives the competitor 30 minutes to charm their worms. You could do the same. Set the clock and start charming using any of these charming methods: push the fork or spade into the ground and bang it to make vibrations; dance all over your plot; drum on the ground with two sticks; use musical instruments to make vibrations; or play your iPod loudly to the grass. What else can you think of?

4 Collect any worms that come to the surface in your bucket. Keep the bucket covered— worms left out in the sun will dry up and die.

5 At the end of half an hour give prizes for the person who has collected:
- the most worms
- the longest worm
- the shortest worm
- the heaviest worm
- the worm with the most segments (the number of rings that make up its body)

caterpillar camouflage

If you could ask a bird what its favorite food was, chances are it would say "Caterpillars!" This isn't great news if you are a caterpillar. So caterpillars use all sorts of different ways to stop being eaten. One of these is camouflage. This means they try to blend in with their surroundings so that they can't be spotted. In this fun game you will find out just how well camouflage works.

You will need

Cardboard

Scissors

Double-sided sticky tape

Scraps of yarn—some brightly colored, some duller greens and brown

1 This game is more fun if you have some friends to play it with and an adult to help. First cut the cardboard into some long rectangles about 8 x 2 in. (20 x 5 cm). They don't have to be perfect. Have one piece for each player.

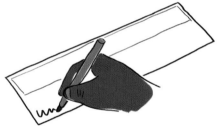

2 Stick a length of double-sided sticky tape along the top of the cardboard. Don't peel off the backing paper yet. Write START at one end of the cardboard.

3 Cut the yarn into 6 in. (15 cm) lengths. Half the pieces should be brightly colored and half should be green or brown—the colors of leaves and branches. These are your caterpillars! It doesn't really matter how many you cut but for a good game you will need about 20 or more. Count them before you begin the game.

4 While you and your friends stay inside, ask the adult to hide all your "caterpillars" in plants, trees, and bushes around your backyard.

SAFETY FIRST
Never touch caterpillars. Many people react badly to them, especially the hairy ones. Always wash your hands after you have been exploring outside.

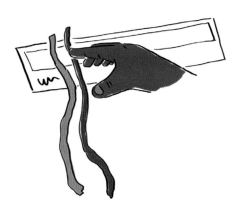

5 Now peel off the backing paper from the sticky tape (this can be a bit tricky) and when the adult says "Ready!", all of you run out and begin searching for the yarn "caterpillars." When you find one, stick it on your cardboard. Stick the first one at the end that says START and line them up in the order in which you find them. Keep going until you have found them all!

6 Count up everyone's caterpillars. If you were birds which of you would have the fullest tummy? Who would still be hungry? Look at the order in which you found your caterpillars. You probably found the bright ones first and the camouflaged ones last. Did you manage to find all the caterpillars or did some survive to turn into butterflies?

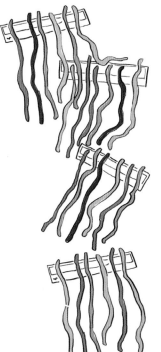

A GAME OF HIDE-AND-SEEK!

10 ways to find out about snails

Snails are fascinating creatures and in this project you are going to investigate them in ten mini-projects. Snails are very easy to find but remember that snails are living things and deserve to be treated gently and with respect, just like any other creature. Also, always remember to wash your hands after you've been exploring outside.

You will need

Large glass jar—take care not to drop it

Plastic wrap (clingfilm)

Elastic band

Pencil

Magnifying glass

Corn starch (cornflour)

Small paintbrush

Plate

Q-tip (cotton bud)

Flashlight (torch)

Vinegar

Sharp knife—ask an adult to help you use this

Small amounts of some of these snail "foods": sawdust, lettuce, oatmeal, apple, milk, cardboard, orange, carrot

Plastic or metal cake box

Sticky tape

Chalk

Brightly colored nail polish

1 Find some snails Snails come out mostly at night but they will still be around on damp, cloudy mornings. On sunny days you will find them hiding in their shells in damp, dark places. Put four or five snails into a large glass jar. Put a few wet leaves and a little damp soil in the jar with them to make them comfortable! To keep them inside, cover the top with plastic wrap (clingfilm). Keep it firm with an elastic band and make a few tiny holes with the point of a pencil to give them air. You will be surprised at how quickly they can escape if you leave the jar open!

2 How do snails move? Take the jar to a cool, shady spot and wait for them to come out of their shells. Watch as a snail crawls up the glass of the jar. Look out for dark ripples moving along its "foot." These are its muscles, which push it along. Look for the trail of slime it leaves as it moves. You may also see it doing a poo as it crawls along! Use the magnifying glass to look closer. Look for a hole near the entrance to its shell. This is the snail's breathing hole.

3 How do snails eat? Mix a little corn starch (cornflour) with some water to make a thin paste. Remove the plastic wrap cover from the jar and use a paintbrush to brush a patch of this paste onto the side of the jar. Watch carefully as the snail eats it—snails love corn starch! Use the magnifying glass to see more clearly. You should be able to see the snail's mouth eating. It has something called a radula, which is like a rough tongue with rows and rows of tiny teeth. It uses the radula to scrape the surface off leaves—a bit like sandpaper. Can you see marks in the corn starch where the radula has scraped?

4 Can snails learn? Take a snail out of the jar and put it on the plate. (Remember to shut the others in!) Wet the Q-tip (cotton bud) and then very gently touch its head behind its tentacles. What happens to the tentacles? How long do they take to come back out again? Leave the snail to move around a bit more, then touch it again. Do this five or six times. After a while you may find that the snail does not take much notice when it is touched. It has learned that nothing bad happens so it is not in danger.

5 Can snails see and hear? Shine the flashlight (torch) at the snail. Does it react? Its upper, longer tentacles react to light and dark, but the snail can't see in the same way as we can. Try whistling or clapping near the snail. Does it react when you make a noise? Snails can't hear so it shouldn't notice the noise you make.

6 Can snails smell? Clean the paintbrush then use it to paint a circle of vinegar around the snail (not too close). Watch what happens as it crawls toward the vinegar. Its lower tentacles can smell. Does it like the smell of vinegar?

7 Why do snails make slime trails? Ask an adult if you can use a sharp knife. Wash the vinegar off the plate and lay the knife flat on the plate. Let the snail crawl onto it (brush on some corn starch paste to tempt it if it doesn't move). When the snail is on the knife, turn the knife so that the sharp blade is facing up and the snail has to climb over it. It sounds cruel but it won't cut the snail! Its slime will protect it. In the wild the slime protects snails from sharp thorns and helps them glide over rough surfaces. It also stops them from drying out.

SNAIL TRAILS AND OTHER SECRETS

8 **What is a snail's favorite food?** Let's find out! Put samples of different foods around the edges of a large plastic box. Include damp sawdust, damp cardboard, lettuce, apple slices, corn starch paste, oatmeal, and a little milk. You could try other fruit and vegetables too but don't include processed sugary or salty foods as these are poisonous to snails. Put all your snails into the middle of the box. Cover the top of the box with plastic wrap, pierce a few tiny holes in the top with a pencil, and hold it down with a large elastic band or some sticky tape. Now wait and watch. Keep checking every few minutes to see which foods the snails end up on. Is there a clear favorite or do all the snails end up on different foods? Leave them overnight. Which foods have been eaten?

9 **Snail race** This part is best done with a few friends. Make a racecourse on a hard surface such as a patio, but make sure you choose a shady, damp corner as snails hate to be dry or out in the sun. Use chalk to draw a large circle and put all the snails in the middle. Each of you should pick a snail. Whose snail will reach the edge first? Can you encourage your snail to go faster or straighter with different foods?

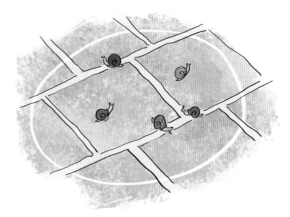

10 **Snail hunt** Gather your snails together—you could perhaps collect some more snails to make this activity even more fun. Mark each snail with a blob of colored nail polish. In the evening, take all the snails to the middle of your backyard and let them go. The next morning, set out for a snail hunt and see how many of your marked snails you can find. How far did they travel in a night? You will probably keep finding your snails over the next weeks, months, or even years as some snails live for a long time! You could also try putting one of your marked snails in your neighbor's yard (you must ask for permission first). You may well find that it has returned to your yard overnight—this is because snails have a homing instinct.

slime safety

Many of the best slime recipes use PVA glue mixed with a borax-based activator. It is the borax in this activator that turns the PVA glue into wonderfully stretchy, squishy, bouncy, flowing slime. In the past, borax powder mixed with water has been used to make slime.

There are some health concerns about borax in slimes. For this reason, we recommend that you use either an eyewash or a contact lens solution which contains boric acid and sodium borate as an activator. Slimes made this way are sometimes described as borax-free; they are not, but contain only very small amounts of borax in a safe form. When using these, you will have to include some baking soda (bicarbonate of soda) in your slime as this reacts with the boric acid and sodium borate to produce the borate ions that make slime possible (see page 20). Borax cannot enter your body through your skin and if you follow our tips below, you shouldn't have any problems.

1. Never try eating any slime (except for the special edible ones made with candies and jello/jelly)—they would taste disgusting anyway.

2. Don't snack while you are making or playing with slime.

3. Keep all PVA slimes away from children under three years of age and also away from pets.

4. If you have any cuts on your hands, cover them with sticky Band-Aids (plasters) and wear latex-free gloves (like the ones doctors use). Always wear latex-free gloves if you have rashes such as eczema on your hands.

5. Keep slimy hands away from your eyes.

6. Wash your hands well after making and playing with slime.

7. Have a special slime-making kit for PVA slimes, which includes bowls, spoons, and measuring cups or pitchers (jugs). Don't use the ones you cook and eat with.

8. Always ask an adult before heating any ingredients to make slime.

9. Always check with an adult before you use any ingredients from the kitchen. Think of playing with PVA slimes as a treat, not an everyday activity. You can play with non-PVA slimes as much as you like.

Index

Index entries in **bold** are experiments

Picture credits

All photography © CICO Books, except for:
© Getty Images: p.7 JGI/Tom Grill; p.41 Peter Muller; p.73 Tetra Images; p.85 Taweesak Baongern EyeEm; p.88 JGI/Jamie Grill